Contents

About this Book

KEY TO SYMBOLS

- map reference to the maps found in the What to See section
- address or location
- telephone number
- opening times
- restaurant or café on premises or near by
- nearest underground train station
- nearest bus/tram route
- nearest overground train station
- ferry crossings and boat excursions
- travel by air
- tourist information
- facilities for visitors with disabilities
- admission charge
- other places of interest near by
- other practical information
- ➤ indicates the page where you will find a fuller description

This book is divided into five sections to cover the most important aspects of your visit to Rhodes.

Viewing Rhodes pages 5–10
An introduction to Rhodes by the author.
The 10 Essentials
The Shaping of Rhodes
Peace and Quiet
Rhodes's Famous

Top Ten pages 11–22
The author's choice of the Top Ten places to see in Rhodes, each with practical information.

What to See pages 23–72
The two main areas of Rhodes, each with its own brief introduction and an alphabetical listing of the main attractions.
Practical information
Snippets of 'Did you know…' information
3 suggested walks
2 suggested drives
2 features

Where To… pages 73–86
Detailed listings of the best places to eat, stay, shop and be entertained.

Practical Matters pages 88–92
A highly visual section containing essential travel information.

Maps
All map references are to the individual maps found in the What to See section of this guide.
For example, Anáktoro ton Arkhónton has the reference 24B2 – indicating the page on which the map is located and the grid square in which the palace is to be found. A list of the maps that have been used in this travel guide can be found in the index.

Prices
Where appropriate, an indication of the cost of an establishment is given by **£** signs:
£££ denotes higher prices, **££** denotes average prices, while **£** denotes lower charges.

Star Ratings
Most of the places described in this book have been given a separate rating:

✪✪✪	Do not miss
✪✪	Highly recommended
✪	Worth seeing

Viewing Rhodes

Above: *the temple of Apollo, Monte Smith*
Right: *an icon painter adds detailed touches to a new work*

Des Hannigan's Rhodes

Rhodes By Any Other Name
The name Rhodes, or Ródos, is said to derive from the story of Helios, the Sun God who spotted Rhodus, the beautiful daughter of Poseidon, beneath the waters of the Mediterranean, and induced her to ascend to the surface with his powerful rays. Another derivation stems from the word *rhodon*, the flower of the pomegranate, a likeness of which appears on ancient Rhodian coins.

On Rhodes you are never too far from beach, bar or boutique, but at every step you move amidst the haunting relics and legacies of the island's vivid past. This is where traces of classical Greece, Byzantium and the Ottoman Empire survive in the medieval Rhodes Old Town and at the exquisite village of Líndos. Rhodes is also the fashionable bustle of its New Town, where the art deco and municipal buildings of the early 20th century merge with the town's modern commercial centre.

The best beach life and nightlife are in the north of the island, at lively resorts such as Faliráki and Ixiá. However, if you travel further south to where the crowds thin out you discover an entirely different island, where rugged pine-clad mountains lie behind long stretches of empty beaches. In the remote interior of Rhodes are quiet villages and hamlets, where time passes unnoticed and where Byzantine churches preserve an atmosphere of utter peace. Few Mediterranean islands can match this mix of indulgent holiday-making and rewarding culture: a world of good food and drink, the promise of escape to nearby islands such as Sými and Chálki, the cool solitude of the mountains, the luxury of hidden coves and the blue Aegean, and the unstinting hospitality of some of the friendliest and most generous people in the world.

A dramatic view of Plateía Ippokrátous (Hippocrates' Square) bathed in the evening light

THE 10 ESSENTIALS

If you only have a short time to visit Rhodes, or would like to get a really complete picture of the island, here are the essentials:

• **Spend time on the less-crowded beaches** of the south and west coasts where you will find open spaces and peace and quiet.

• **Wander through Rhodes Old Town** (➤ 18 and ➤ 36). Take your time and make several visits in order to absorb fully the wonderful atmosphere.

• **Find out if there is a festival or cultural event** being held during your stay and if there is, join in (➤ 86).

• **Visit ancient Kameíros** (➤ 16) **and Líndos** (➤ 57). Both transcend their picture-postcard images. Try to visit as early in the day as possible, when they are less crowded.

• **Spend time in Rhodes New Town** (➤ 34) and enjoy the atmosphere of modern, cosmopolitan Greece in cafés and restaurants, and in the fashionable shops.

• **Head for the mountains** and spend time in villages such as Monólithos (➤ 20), Siána (➤ 64) or Émponas (➤ 46).

• **Always take time to relax at *kafenío* (coffee shop) tables.** Watch the world go by, but make lively conversation as well.

• **Try to fit in an overnight stay on the island of Sými** (➤ 68). A day trip is rewarding, but Sými's old town of Chorió, all steep stone staircases and twisting alleys, is best enjoyed in the cool of evening.

• **Explore some of Rhodes' farming villages** such as Lárdos (➤ 56), Triánta (➤ 66) or Archángelos (➤ 44). You'll catch the down-to-earth flavour of everyday Rhodes.

• **Eat and drink Greek.** Try a selection of *mezédhes* (starters) – a good selection can make a superb meal in itself. If you enjoy wine, then try the excellent Rhodian vintages.

Top: *the long expanse of sand and shingle beach at Afántou Bay*
Above: *dining in the open air at an Old Town restaurant*

A bottle of red wine, produced locally on the island

The Shaping of Rhodes

6000 BC
Natural harbours, such as those at Líndos, are probably used by late Stone Age traders from the nearby mainland.

2000–500 BC
Rhodian harbours are exploited by Phoenicians, and Minoans from Crete.

411 BC
Líndos, Ialyssós and Kameíros unite in establishing a capital city of classical elegance .

***c*290 BC**
Creation of enormous bronze statue, the Colossus of Rhodes

200 BC
Roman influence over Dodecanese begins.

AD 57
St Paul brings Christianity to Rhodes.

100–1000
Rhodes is attacked by Goths, Saracens, Venetians, Franks and Genoese. Culture and religion remain under Byzantine influence.

1309
Rhodes is taken over by the Knights of the Order of St John of Jerusalem. The Knights rule the island for 213 years.

1522
The Turkish Sultan, Souleïmán I (The Magnificent) lays siege to Rhodes. The surviving Knights surrender after 145 days and negotiate their retreat from the island. Turkish rule lasts for nearly 400 years.

1912–43
Italian occupation of the Dodecanese Islands. New building and restoration of archaeological sites; construction of grandiose civic buildings, roads, model farms and irrigation schemes.

1943–5
German occupation of Rhodes.

1945–7
United Nations' Trusteeship of the Dodecanese.

1948
Rhodes and the rest of the Dodecanese reunited with Greece.

1988
Rhodes Old Town declared a UNESCO World Heritage Site.

2000
Rhodian authorities announce plan for a recreated Colossus.

The evocative ruins at Kameíros

Peace & Quiet

On Rhodes there is a noticeable thinning out of development south of Líndos and Kalavárdha on the east and west coasts respectively. In the far south there are uncrowded beaches. Venturing inland offers a refreshing chance to escape into the forested mountains of the central west coast, where there is an almost sub-alpine element to the landscape.

Rodhiní Park

You can find areas of leafy shade and an escape from the often crowded streets of Rhodes Town in Rodhiní Park, a pleasant wooded enclave of cypresses, maples, pines and oleanders, with a stream running through it. The park lies 3km south of the town centre on the road to Líndos. Within the park is a compound containing the surviving herd of Rhodian deer.

Walking

The best areas for walking are in the mountains, but there are no detailed maps available and it can be difficult planning routes that do not involve long sections of roads. There are a number of trails, many of which lead to remote chapels, and these are usually signed with paint marks on rocks. The island of Sými is well supplied with waymarked paths and tracks, but be aware that the terrain can be very dry and rugged.

Flora and Fauna

Many areas of the countryside are clothed in *maquis*, a mix of low-growing Kermes oak and mastic trees, shrubs such as juniper, gorse, and tree heather, and a colourful spread of resilient flowering plants such as rosemary and rock rose. On the more arid mountain slopes and coastal strips species include juniper, spiny burnet and a variety of aromatic herbs. The flowering season is from late February to May/June, after which not much survives the searing heat. In spring and early summer, look out for such vivid plants as the pink-flowered Judas Tree, white and pink cyclamen, ink-blue irises, and blood-red poppies.

Spare that Tree
Rhodes's natural woodland is made up of a mix of Calabrian and Aleppo pine, cypress and evergreen oak. Disastrous forest fires, many allegedly the work of ruthless arsonism by unscrupulous would-be developers, have robbed the island of substantial areas of woodland. Much precious forest remains however, especially in the mountainous west.

Below: *colourful mesembryanthemums are found all over the island*
Bottom: *the countryside near Apóllona*

Rhodes's Famous

Colossus of Rhodes

The Colossus of Rhodes was one of the seven wonders of the ancient world. Completed in 290 or 292 BC, the 34m-high bronze statue was said to be of the Sun God Helios. It was fashioned as a memorial of Rhodes's resistance to the prolonged and savage siege of the city by the Macedonian king Demetrios. The huge statue took twelve years to construct and is said to have been designed by a sculptor from Líndos called Chares. The claim that the Colossus was positioned with its legs bridging the entrance to Mandraki Harbour was probably the result of later myth-making. It is more likely that the figure stood in the vicinity of the harbour, probably within the castle walls. In 227 BC the Colossus was toppled by a massive earthquake that shattered the statue into pieces.

The Knights of St John
The Knights of the Order of St John of Jerusalem were key figures in the history of Rhodes. The Knights were formed in Jerusalem in the 11th century, their purpose being to care for the sick and to protect pilgrims from the infidel. The Knights developed into a powerful military and commercial organisation and fought in the Crusades.
In 1291 they retreated from Palestine to Cyprus and then in 1309 to Rhodes, where they bought – and fought – their way onto the island.
For the next 213 years the Knights dominated island life, enriching themselves through trade and through thinly veiled piracy, until a final massive siege by Turkish forces led to the Order withdrawing, eventually to Malta.

Lawrence Durrell

The English novelist Lawrence Durrell was a devoted Graecophile, who came to Rhodes in June 1945 to take up an appointment as Public Information Officer for the Dodecanese Islands. He lived for a time in a small house in the old Muslim graveyard adjoining the Mosque of Mourad Reïs (➤ 39). Durrell named the house, rather grandly, as The Villa Cleobolus, after the ruler of ancient Líndos (➤ 59). The house survives today, though in a rather dilapidated state.

Durrell lived on Rhodes until March 1947 and wrote about his experiences in his book *Reflections on a Marine Venus.*

Top Ten

Above: *a detail of a mosaic depicting the Nine Muses, in the Palace of the Grand Masters*
Right: *this slender minaret is a highlight of a walk around the Old Town*

1

Anáktoro ton Arkhónton (Palace of the Grand Masters)

 24B2

Plateía Kleovoulou

0241 23359

Apr–Oct, Tue–Sun 8.30–7. Nov–Mar, Tue–Sun 8:30–3 (hours can be flexible, especially during peak season)

Café on site (££)

Few

Moderate, free on Sun

Old Town Walls (➤ 38), Ippotón (➤ 15)

The Palace of the Grand Masters is an impressive monumental building, a 1930s Italian reconstruction of the medieval original.

The 15th-century Knights of St John built their Palace of the Grand Masters on the roots of a decaying Byzantine fortress. The building remained the focus of the Collachium, the inner fortress of the Knights, until the Turkish conquest of 1522. In 1856 the palace was demolished by an accidental explosion of stored munitions. It was a sorry ruin that the Italians tried to recreate in its medieval form; although their choice of materials proved to be less than durable, and their methods less than responsible. Numerous ancient artefacts were dumped in the new foundations.

Today the palace houses two outstanding museum collections on its ground floor: the Museum of Ancient Rhodes (➤ 33) and the Medieval Exhibition (➤ 31). From the cool shade of the palace's entrance portal, you emerge into the harsh, almost brutal, white light of the inner courtyard; it is lined with cloisters and arches, some holding Hellenistic statues, transferred from Kos by the Italians. Marble well-heads mark the sites of the original grain silos of the Knights. A grand staircase leads from the left of the entrance portal to a circuit of upper chambers, paved with exquisite Hellenistic, Roman and early Christian mosaics and marble inlays, also from Kos. Look for superb examples in the Chamber of the Sea Horse and Nymph, in the Dolphin Chamber, and in the corridor where Poseidon defeats the giant Polybotes.

Right: *the imposing entrance to the palace*
Below: *the cloistered inner courtyard*

2
Asklipeío

The remote inland village of Asklipeío boasts two splendid Byzantine monuments: the Church of the Dormition of the Virgin, and the castle ruins.

The superb church dates from 1060, and was built over an existing basilica. Its cruciform shape is supplemented by two additional apses. Built of warm, honey-coloured stone with a red-tiled dome and barrel roofs, there is a separate belltower gateway. Inside the church is a feast of 17th-century frescoes, as fine as any you'll see on Rhodes. The frescoes are narrative in style and illustrate Old Testament themes such as the Genesis sequence and the story of Daniel and the Lion. The splendid *hokhláki* (pebble mosaic) floor has a big star motif in front of the altar, and from the central dome there hangs a truly awesome chandelier. Alongside the church are two small museums, one displaying religious items, the other a collection of rural artefacts including oil pressing equipment.

A signposted road leads up to the castle from whose ruinous battlements there are fine views across the inland *maquis*-smothered hills and east towards the sea. The castle is well protected by natural rock outcrops, and by jagged fangs of rock that would have formed a natural barrier in their own right. The interior of the castle is overgrown, and you may stumble on the occasional carcass of sheep or goat. There is a narrow inner parapet round the walls, and ruinous water tanks, sunk into the ground, are in an unprotected condition.

Above: *the cross-shaped design of the Church of the Dormition of the Virgin reflects its origins as a basilica, over which the 11th-century church was built*

42B2

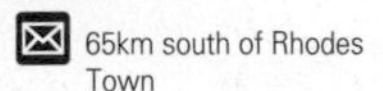

65km south of Rhodes Town

Church, daily 9–1, 5–7 (irregular opening in winter). Services are held at various times. Museums, same hours as church. Castle, open access

Agapitos Taverna (£)

East side bus, Rhodes–Asklipeío, daily (Rimini Sq)

Good at church, none at castle

Church and museums free (donations welcomed), castle free

Gennádi (► 48), Glystra (► 49), Kiotári (► 50)

Saint's Day Festival, 15 Aug. Please do not enter church wearing shorts or revealing tops. Avoid casual visits during services

3
Ialyssós

- 43D5
- 10km southwest of Rhodes Town
- Apr–Oct, Tue–Sun 8–7, Mon 8–2:30. Nov–Mar, Tue–Sun 8:30–3
- Café/shop on site (££)
- West side bus, Rhodes–Paradissi, daily (Averof St), to Triánta only
- None
- Moderate
- Triánta (➤ 66)

The ancient city of Ialyssós once stood on the slopes of 267m-high Mt Filérimos. Today the site contains outstanding archaeological artefacts.

The golden-walled Church of Our Lady was built originally by the Knights of St John, and was restored during the early 20th century by the Italians. Internally, it is an exquisite cluster of cool hexagonal chambers, each with groin vaulting. Behind the church is a colonnaded courtyard with monastic cells, linked to a two-storeyed abbot's quarters. In front of the church's handsome bell tower is a sunken baptismal font dating from a 5th–6th century Christian basilica. Immediately outside the church's entrance door lie the excavated foundations of a 3rd century BC Temple of Athena, successor to an even earlier Phoenician temple. It is the most poignant feature of the hilltop, and offers a tantalising indication of what else may lie buried here.

Beyond all this lie the cliff-edge ruins of a Byzantine fortress that was used in turn by the Knights of St John, the Turks and the Italians, and then was bombed by Allied forces during World War II. Among other features on Filérimos is the chapel of Ágios Georgios Hostos, sunk into the hillside just to the left of the entrance booth. The chapel contains rather faded, but still impressive, medieval frescoes. To the west of the café, an Italian-era 'Calvary' avenue, hooded by trees and flanked by rather grim Stations of the Cross, leads arrow-straight to a monumental cross, 17m high and with an internal staircase leading to viewing areas in the cross's arms.

The church's bell tower stands above the remains of a 5th century baptismal font

4

Ippotón (Street of the Knights)

The famous 'medieval' street of Ippotón is a set-piece Italian restoration of the enclave created by the Knights of St John as their main thoroughfare.

Ippotón is a beautiful urban street, a portrait in warm stone and close-knit cobbling. It descends to the east from the entrance gate of the Palace of the Grand Masters and has a formal stillness that is barely relieved during the day by clusters of visitors listening with hushed intent to their tour guides. The buildings contain splendid interiors, but most are occupied by municipal and cultural organisations and are not open to the public, unless by special arrangement. Absence of commercial outlets has preserved the street's architectural integrity, but its modern appearance gives no flavour of its probable medieval vigour and messiness. The Knights kept their horses in ground floor stables here.

The Knights were organised by their countries of origin and by their language into national groups called 'Tongues'. Each Tongue had its own establishment or 'Inn' where meetings were held and where guests were accommodated. Many of the Inns are located in Ippotón, including the Inns of Provence and of Spain and the impressive Inn of the Tongue of France, located about midway down the north side of the street. This building is notable for its arched doorways, turreted battlements and crocodile waterspouts. Throughout the street, marble reliefs displaying coats of arms disturb the flat rigour of the buildings' facades. Here and there, dim alleyways lead off from the south side of Ippotón towards the commercial frenzy of the neighbouring shopping street of Sokratous, a striking contrast to the hush of Ippotón.

25C2

Rhodes Old Town

Open access

Several cafés in Orfeos at west end (£–££)

Few

Palace of the Grand Masters (► 12)

Above: *Looking down the Street of the Knights from the entrance gate to the Palace of the Grand Masters*

5

Kameíros

42B4

34km southwest of Rhodes Town

0241 40037/75674

Apr–Oct 8–7, Nov–Mar 8:30–4.30. Closed Mon

Seasonal café (££), tavernas (£) at coast road access

West side bus, Rhodes–Kameíros, daily (Averof St), to coast road turnoff only. 1km uphill to site

Few, but good overview of site from surrounding levels and paths

Moderate

The archaelogical remains at Kameíros ascend a terraced hillside, set against the blue ocean

Ancient Kameíros is one of the most pleasing ruins of Mediterranean antiquity, reflecting a period when Greek civilisation was at its apogee.

Kameíros has an idyllic location on a pine-covered hillside above the sea. The settlement probably originated in the 2nd millennium BC, but flourished during the period 1000–400 BC. It was devastated by an earthquake in 226 BC, but was rebuilt. A later earthquake in AD 142 led to a final abandonment. Kameíros is a glorious reminder of the balance and serenity of urban planning in Hellenistic Greece, and is a persuasive argument in favour of the period being designated a true 'Golden Age'.

The site lies within a south-facing terraced amphitheatre, partially excavated from a hillside. The central street rises from the lowest area of public buildings round Agorá Square. These buildings included an *agorá*, or market building, Doric and Ionic temples, a sanctuary with altars, a bath house, and Fountain Square, with its columns partially restored. The level above is filled with the ruins of houses, units of which are separated by narrow alleyways. To the right, a restored stone staircase leads up from the public area to the upper level, where the Acropolis was sited and where the foundations of a sacred precinct, a temple and a *stoa* (collonaded avenue) survive. Try to visit early or late in the day, to avoid the large number of coach parties that arrive by late morning.

6
Líndos Acropolis

Situated on a spectacular hill, the Acropolis is a potent mix of ancient Greek antiquities and Byzantine and medieval buildings.

This rocky outcrop above Líndos was a perfect spot for fortifications

The 114m-high Acropolis hill of Líndos dominates the coast to north and south. The low-lying neck of land behind the Acropolis sparkles with the white-painted houses of the medieval village of Líndos (➤ 57). The Sanctuary of Athena Lindia was established on the Acropolis in the 2nd millennium BC and today is one of its finest restorations. Later additions included a large *stoa* (colonnaded avenue), vaults and cisterns. Substantial fortifications were added during the Byzantine period, as was the Church of St John that stands inside the Acropolis.

Stones from the ancient structures were used by the Knights of St John to repair and expand the Byzantine fortress. The Italians carried out substantial reconstruction during the early 20th century, but their methods and materials were often inadequate, and today there is a continuing refurbishment that accounts for the often frustrating presence of scaffolding and machinery. Make your way up the approach path past the souvenir sellers, and take a deep breath before you tackle the steep approach steps. Pick your way carefully through the darkened vault of the Knights' Hall, climb in brilliant sunlight to the terrace and up the monumental staircase, then wander amidst this glorious open-air museum of Aegean history, with superb views as a bonus.

- 43C2
- 56km south of Rhodes Town
- 0244 31258/0241 75674
- May–Oct, Tue–Sun 8–6:40, Mon 12.30–6:40. Nov–Apr, Tue–Sun 8:30–2:40
- Snack bar at entrance (££)
- East side bus, Rhodes–Líndos, daily (Rimini Sq)
- Summer excursion ferries daily from Mandraki Harbour
- Main Square, Líndos
- None
- Moderate
- Líndos (➤ 57)

7
Medieval Town of Rhodes

25C2

Numerous cafés, restaurants and tavernas (£–£££)

Tourist information: Papagou St 0241 23655

Few

Pre-Lenten carnival (➤ 86)

Rhodes Old Town is a medieval fortress town of such historical value that it was declared a World Heritage Site by UNESCO in 1988.

The Old Town of Rhodes is contained within the 4km of defensive walls that the Knights of St John built on Byzantine fortifications. Within the walls lie remains of Hellenistic, Roman, Byzantine and Moorish buildings, all locked within a medieval warren of lanes and alleyways. The Knights divided their city into two enclaves. In the higher northwestern section lay the Collachium, the castle, in which stood the Palace of the Grand Masters, the administrative buildings and dwellings of the Order. The rest of the town was the Hora, or Burg, where the merchants and working population lived.

Today the Collachium incorporates the carefully preserved monumental buildings of the Knights, impressive, but slightly sterile, museum pieces. It is the Hora, the Lower Town, that captivates with its dark sandstone and limestone buildings, occasional walls vivid with ochre and sea blue paint, and all crammed within a tangled web of cobbled lanes, many of which are braced

throughout their lengths with flying arches intended to minimise earthquake damage. Everywhere, tree-shaded squares and courtyards punctuate the maze. No building replicates another amidst this marvellous scrabble of jostling houses, dilapidated mosques, tiny Byzantine churches, ancient foundations, ornamental doorways, *hokhláki* (pebble mosaic) paving and dusty lost corners.

Ten gates in the encircling walls give access from the New Town and harbour areas to this marvellous enclave. The monumental areas of Ippotón (➤ 15) and the Palace of the Grand Masters (➤ 12) are easily explored, but while wandering through the Old Town it can be easy to miss some outstanding corners. More selective areas to search out are the ancient streets of Omírou, Ippodámou, Pythagora, and especially the enchanting Ágios Fanoúriou, with its attendant network of arched alleyways. A walk along the Old Town walls is recommended (➤ 38) for an overview of the dense jigsaw of buildings, backyards, and alleyways and the spectacular defensive works of the outer walls and moat (➤ 37).

The Old Jewish Quarter (➤ 35) occupies the most easterly section of the Old Town and is often the busiest area. It is the first stop for cruise ship visitors and leads seamlessly into the thronging Sokratous Street, the Old Town's shopping mall. Even the crowds of tourists cannot detract from the absorbing fascination of the Old Town. All those competing tavernas and restaurants, cafés, souvenir shops, and the chattering bottlenecks of popular shopping areas are entirely in keeping with the Old Town's centuries of raucous commercial life.

Left: *looking out over the Old Town from the encircling walls*
Top: *a series of arches characterising a street in the Old Town*
Above: *doors to the synagogue, with painted-over Star of David motifs*

8

Monólithos

This spectacular medieval castle, perched high on a rocky pinnacle, offers superb views over a landscape of forested mountains and wild coastline.

42A3

On the west coast, 55km southwest of Rhodes Town

Open access

Seasonal *kantiná* (food and drink stall) at approach to castle and Fourni beach (£)

West side bus, Rhodes–Monólithos, daily (Averof St), to Monólithos village only

None

Free

Siána (➤ 64)

Above: *the 15th-century castle of Monólithos dominates its forbidding rock base*

The castle of Monólithos stands on top of an enormous crag called Monopetra that rises to a height of 236m from pine-covered slopes above Kerameni Bay. The castle dates from 1476 and was a stronghold of the Knights of St John, built on top of an existing Byzantine fortress. Its broken walls shelter a ruined basilica and the intact church of St Panteleimon. The castle is easily reached from roadside parking by following a path that leads through pines to a fine stone staircase. The seaward side of the rock plunges for 200m, so take great care when near the edge. There are exhilarating views of the island of Chálki (➤ 45) and of the coast to the north.

The road leading on from the castle descends for 5km through an astonishing series of bends to reach the remote, south-facing Fourni beach. On the east side of a projecting rock headland, reached by rough steps and a path from the far end of the beach, are man-made caves, probably carved out by fishermen at some time in the past but also said to have contained ancient burials, and now revered as holy grottoes. Steps lead down to a sea washed pit, known locally as The Queen's Bath, but more probably an old sluice-pot, used by fishermen for storing shellfish. The nearby village of Monólithos is an unassuming, friendly place with a long history of survival against the odds, including strong resistance to the German occupation of 1943–5.

9
Petaloúdes

Petaloúdes is Rhodes' famous 'Valley of the Butterflies' where swarms of Jersey tiger moths settle each summer in order to breed.

Petaloúdes is a relentlessly popular tourist destination that attracts vast numbers of coach tours and individual visitors as much as it does its moths; or 'butterflies' as they are called for publicity reasons. The moths gather at Petaloúdes from late June to September, attracted by the shade and humidity of the stream-fed woods and by the resin of the numerous liquid amber trees in the valley. They cover the trunks of the trees and the surfaces of stream side rocks with a cloak of yellow and black wings, relieved by occasional blinks of red underwing.

Petaloúdes lies in a wooded fold of the hills that run southwest from Rhodes Town. The path through the upper and lower valley is landscaped, surfaced, railed off and linked by rustic bridges and stairways. Conspicuous signs, and an increased control by the site management, remind visitors that disturbance of the moths is stressful to them and can disrupt the mating cycle.

43C4

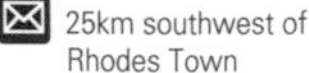
25km southwest of Rhodes Town

0241 91998

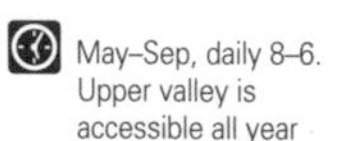
May–Sep, daily 8–6. Upper valley is accessible all year

Taverna/cafés on site (££)

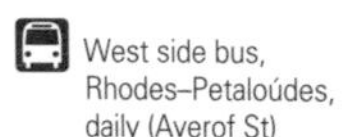
West side bus, Rhodes–Petaloúdes, daily (Averof St)

Few

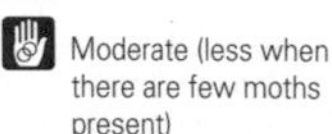
Moderate (less when there are few moths present)

Outside the main 'butterfly' months of June to September, the valley is still a pleasantly wooded escape from the beaches and the sun's glare, even although the main attraction is absent. At any time of the year, the valley above the upper road offers a pleasant uphill walk of just under 1km to the little monastery church of Panagía Kalópetra on the road above.

Pathways are designed to provide access for tourists, but also to minimise disturbance to the moths' habitat

10
Profítis Ilías

42B4

50km southwest of Rhodes Town

Open access

Seasonal *kafenío* (£)

West side bus, Rhodes–Salakos, daily (Averof St). There is a steep path leading up to Profítis Ilías from Salakos. Allow 1½ hours.

None

Feast of Profítis Ilías, 20 Jul. The area is very popular on *Kathari Deftera*, 'Clean Monday', the Monday before Ash Wednesday

The church and its frescoes were endowed by a father whose children had died; it is dedicated to St Nicholas, protector of children

The wooded mountain of Profítis Ilías rises to a height of 798m and there are magnificent views of the island from the top.

Today Profítis Ilías is a forested enclave with a mix of mainly Calabrian pines, cedars and oaks. In the 1930s, the Italian occupiers of the island set about transforming the forested ridge of the mountain into a semi-wild park, attracted perhaps by the sub-Alpine nature of the terrain. The ruins and remains of this era are a telling comment on the fate of fascist ambition, yet much of the Italian landscaping still enhances Profítis Ilías in contrast to the ugly clusters of communication aerials and buildings that crowd its off-limits summit.

The road that climbs the mountain's wooded slopes from Sálakos in the west is a serpentine delight (➤ 55). If you approach from Eleoússa in the east, you pass the charming little Byzantine church of Ágios Nikólaos Fountoúkli in its peaceful roadside setting. The church contains some fine, if faded, medieval frescoes. Both approaches lead eventually to a junction, high amidst the pines, but below the true summit. Here stands the Italian era, chalet-style hotel Elafos and its annexe, Elafina. The complex is no longer used. Alongside is the Church of Profítis Ilías. There is car parking by the old hotel and at the roadside near the old stable building which now houses a *kafenío* (café/coffee shop). A rough track leads higher up the mountain, but there are old pathways through the woods that make for enjoyable walking (➤ 47).

What to See

Above: *fresco with ornate surround, Kattavía*
Right: *the broken capital of an ancient column makes a useful wash basin*

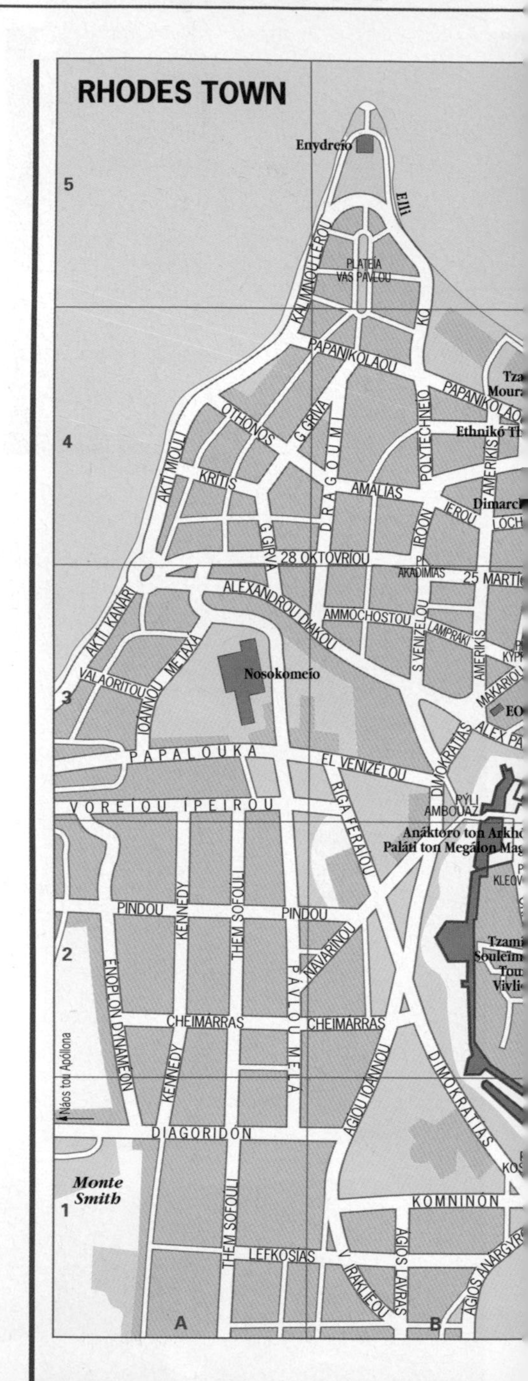
RHODES TOWN
Enydreío
Ellis
PLATEÍA
VAS PAVLOU
KALIMNOU LEROU
PAPANIKOLAOU
OTHONOS
G GRIVA
DRAGOUMI
POLYTECHNEIO
AMERIKIS
AKTI MIOULI
KRITIS
AMALÍAS
IEROU
IROON
G GIRVA
28 OKTOVRIOU
AKADIMÍAS
25 MARTÍ
ALÉXANDROU DIAKOU
AMMÓCHOSTOU
LAMPRAKI
S VENIZÉLOU
AKTI KANARI
VALAORITOU
IOANNOU METAXA
Nosokomeío
MAKARIOU
DIMOKRATÍAS
PAPALOUKA
EL VENIZÉLOU
VOREIOU ÍPEIROU
RÍGA FERAÍOU
PÝLI
AMBOUAZ
PINDOU
KENNEDY
THEM SOFOULI
NAVARINOU
ÉNOPLON DYNAMEÓN
PÁVLOU MELA
CHEIMÁRRAS
ÁGIOU IOANNOU
DIMOKRATÍAS
Náos tou Apóllona
DIAGORIDON
Monte
Smith
KOMNINÓN
LEFKOSÍAS
IRAKLÍEOU
ÁGIOS LAVRAS
ÁGIOS ANARGYR
5
4
3
2
1
A
B

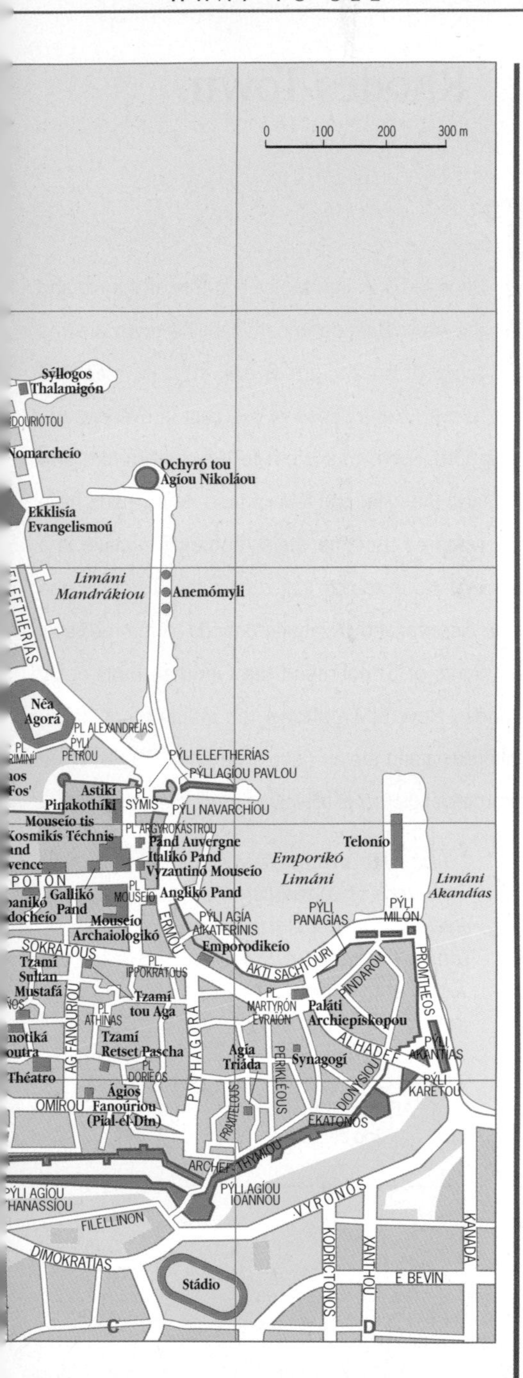

PL = Plateía, meaning square

The word for street, odos, has been omitted from the map

Rhodes Town

Rhodes Town is a captivating mix of the old and the new. Buried beneath today's town are the roots of an ancient Greek city, its classical elegance lost forever. Yet a sense of the past is everywhere. The surviving Old Town has weathered earthquake and bombardment and the wear and tear of time. Many parts have been heavily restored, but the main medieval enclave is a fascinating mix of old buildings that reflect the history of the town from the classical and Byzantine periods to the medieval eras of the Knights of St John and the Ottoman Empire. By contrast, Rhodes New Town shows the influence of Italian monumental building and the art deco style of the 1930s, while the main commercial district is a lively modern precinct.

'The eyes could never have enough of watching the circle of the walls and their lofty and beautiful towers, looking straight as candles to those approaching from the sea.'

AELIUS ARISTEIDES
2nd century BC

Rhodes Town can keep you busy and entertained for days. It is the duality of the place that makes it so compelling: the fascinating contrast of the Old Town with the emphatically modern New Town. The defensive walls that the Knights of St John built on a monumental scale ensured the Old Town's survival as a distinctive enclave compared with the changing world outside.

As soon as you enter the Old Town through any of the handsome gates that punctuate its walls, you feel the difference. Within lie museums and galleries, and a huge variety of cafés, tavernas and restaurants, all within the framework of a medieval city.The harbours were the key to the success of ancient Rhodes, and today they are a link between the old and the new. At Mandraki, with its old windmills and lines of expensive motor cruisers, yachts and colourful local ferries, you enter modern Rhodes, a world of frantic traffic along the harbourside Eleftherías Street. However, the pedestrianised quayside also means that you can relax and watch the world sail by, while just across the way is the bustling New Market and behind it the busy heart of the New Town. Here you will find, alongside fashion shops crammed with Europe's leading brands, mouth-watering delicatessens and relaxed café terraces.

Extensive selection (£–£££)

Town buses from opposite entrance to New Market (Néa Agorá)

Excursion boats leave from Mandraki Harbour; inter-island ferries from Commercial Harbour

Greek National Tourist Organisation, corner Makariou/Papagou Sts; City of Rhodes Tourist Information, Rimini Sq; seasonal openings

Below: *ruined church, Old Town*
Bottom: *yachts, Mandraki harbour*

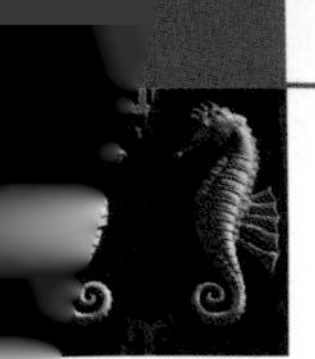

What to See in Rhodes Town

ANÁKTORO TON ARKHÓNTON – PALACE OF THE GRAND MASTERS (► 12, TOP TEN)

ASTIKI PINAKOTHIKI (MUNICIPAL ART GALLERY) ✪✪

The Municipal Art Gallery is housed in the upper level of an attractive medieval-style building and contains one of the finest collections of modern Greek art in existence. The gallery was founded in 1962 by Andreas Ioannou, the then Prefect of the Dodecanese. The substantial collection, not all of which is on show at any one time, covers various periods from 1863 to the 1940s and gives a rich insight to the development of modern Greek painting.

- 25C3
- 2 Symis Square, Old Town
- 0241 23766/36646
- Mon–Sat 8–2
- Neorion Café, Mandraki Quay (£)
- None
- Cheap
- Museum of Decorative Arts (► 32)

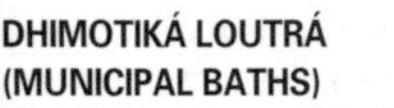

DHIMOTIKÁ LOUTRÁ (MUNICIPAL BATHS) ✪

The *hammam*, or Turkish bath, is the most tangible legacy of nearly 300 years of Turkish influence on Rhodes. Known officially as the Municipal Baths, the much renovated *hammam* is one of only two such working complexes in Greece. The exterior of the building is unremarkable, but inside are all the hallmarks of Moorish hydromechanics – underfloor pipes that carry the water which is heated by olive wood fires – side chambers with

- 25C2
- Aríonos Square, Old Town
- 0241 27739
- Tue 1–6, Wed–Sat 11–5.30
- To Diafani, Aríonos Square (£)
- Few
- Cheap (slightly more expensive Tue–Fri)
- No photography allowed

Above: *this dashing, moustachioed figure can be seen in the Art Gallery*
Right: *looking across the west beach towards the aquarium*

wash sinks and marble floor slabs, and the star-pierced dome above the central hot room. There are male and female sections (bathers go naked) and the baths are kept very clean. Wooden slippers are supplied but bring your own towel.

ELLI BEACH ✪

Beaches of variable quality lie to either side of the most northerly tip of Rhodes' New Town. The long, west-facing beach is backed by a busy ring road and it can be very windy, thus proving more amenable to windsurfers than to sun-worshippers. The more sheltered Elli Beach on the eastern side of the headland is a long crescent of shingle that sets off the banks of luxury hotels dominating the shoreline. Crowds of sunbathers are the price of Elli being a town beach and it gets very busy in peak season. You can escape to an offshore diving platform, often just as busy, but check depth before diving. All types of beach furniture and watersports are available.

- 24B5
- Kos St
- Cafés and snack bars along beachfront (£–££)
- Few
- Aquarium (➤ below)

ENYDREÍO (AQUARIUM) ✪

The Italian-era Aquarium stands in a breezy location on Ammos Point at the most northerly tip of Rhodes Town. This appealing building is a monument to 1930s art deco, right down to the seahorse and seashell reliefs on the doorcase. The building is an outstation of the Greek National Centre for Marine Research and a great deal of research work is carried out. Famed for some of its embalmed museum *grotesques* such as a ferociously leathery Mako shark, the true aquarium is housed in the basement and contains a number of sea-fed tanks displaying various Aegean species of fish, mammals and marine organisms.

- 24B5
- Kos St
- 0241 27308; fax 0241 78321
- Apr–Oct, daily 9–9. Nov–Mar, daily 9–4:30
- Cafés at Elli Beach (£–££)
- Few
- Moderate
- Elli Beach (➤ above)
- Aquarium is being renovated so check opening hours

IPPOTÓN – STREET OF THE KNIGHTS (➤ 15, TOP TEN)

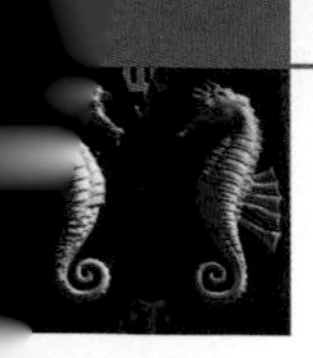

- 25C3
- New Town
- Kon Tiki (££), Mandraki; Akteon Café (££), Plateía Eleftherías
- Few
- Medieval Town (➤ 18), New Town (➤ 34)

LIMÁNI MANDRÁKIOU (MANDRAKI HARBOUR) ✪✪

The attractive Mandraki Harbour is the most northerly of Rhodes' three harbours and by far the most interesting. This was the ancient 'sheep pen', the name in Greek being *mandri*, a name often used for small, encircling harbours. Mandraki was one of the five ports of ancient Rhodes. It was the naval port and was known as the 'small harbour' as opposed to the 'great harbour', the present Commercial Harbour. The entrance to ancient Mandraki could be sealed with chains. Legend claims that the harbour entrance was spanned by the legendary Colossus of Rhodes (➤ 10), but there is no proof of this. Today twin columns bearing statues of Rhodian deer, a stag and doe, stand on either side of the harbour gap. A row of restored medieval windmills, symbols of the days when corn was ground at the harbourside, stands along the outer quay. At the seaward end of the quay is the fortress of St Nicholas, built in the 1460s and now the site of a lighthouse. On its landward side the harbour is bordered by the busy Eleftherías Street, at the end of which is Plateía Vasileos Georgiou I. Here the Italians left a collection of interesting monumental buildings in a mix of Venetian, Gothic and Moorish architectural styles. On the quayside stands the Ekklisía Evangelismoú, the Cathedral of St John the Evangelist.

This stag, guarding one side of the harbour, is mirrored by a doe on the opposite side

DID YOU KNOW?

The statues of deer that stand at Mandraki Harbour's entrance depict a special breed, said to have been introduced in classical times in a bid to combat a plague of snakes. Suggestions are that the deer ate the snakes, trampled them, or that the snakes were fatally infected by the deer's droppings.

MEDIEVAL EXHIBITION

The Medieval Exhibition is housed in wings of the Palace of the Grand Masters (► 12) and gives a vivid insight into the Byzantine, medieval and Turkish periods of Rhodes's long history. The commercial and trading history of the Byzantine period is well illustrated and there are fascinating depictions of how the town has developed, and indeed contracted, since its Hellenistic inception. Other exhibits portray the life and times of the Knights of St John and there are displays of manuscripts and icons.

24B2
Palace of the Grand Masters, Kleovoulou Square
0241 23359; fax 0241 31048
Apr–Oct, Tue–Sun 8–7, Mon 12–7. Nov–Mar, Tue–Sun 8:30–3
Café inside Palace (££)
Few
Moderate – included in entry fee to Palace
Ippotón (► 15)

MEDIEVAL TOWN OF RHODES (► 18, TOP TEN)

MONTE SMITH

The name Monte Smith (after the British admiral Sydney Smith) has usurped the Greek name for the 112m hill that overlooks Rhodes Town. The hilltop was the religious and ceremonial focus of the magnificent 5th-century BC city of Rhodes that fanned out in geometrical elegance below its eastern escarpment. On the summit stood temples and monuments, but earthquakes and subsequent neglect did much to efface all their architectural glory. The Italians partially restored a 3rd-century BC Temple of Apollo, of which only a cluster of columns survives. At the bottom of the escarpment is an Italian restoration of a theatre and stadium that retain just a few original fragments.

24A1
2km west of New Town
Open access
No 5 bus to Agios Ioannis, every 40 mins from opposite New Market entrance
None (the hilltop site is flat, but uneven)
Ixiá (► 49)

The remains of the Temple of Apollo

25C2
Mouseío Square, Old Town
0241 31048/79601
Daily 8:30–2:30 (may stay open later in peak season)
Cafés in Ermou St (££)
None
Moderate
Ippotón (➤ 15), Byzantine Museum (➤ 33), Museum of Decorative Arts (➤ below)

MOUSEÍO ARCHAIOLOGIKÓ (ARCHAEOLOGICAL MUSEUM)

Rhodes' Archaeological Museum is located in the old Hospital of the Knights, a rather severe, but impressive, 15th-century Gothic building. A steep staircase leads to the magnificent infirmary hall with its central colonnade, the capitals of which are carved with heraldic devices. The smaller side chambers of the upper gallery contain some fine artefacts including the celebrated, yet unglamorous, Marine Venus, a sea-eroded 4th-century BC statue of Aphrodite, that inspired the novelist Lawrence Durrell (➤ 10). In other chambers are superb Rhodian amphorae, some fine Attic pottery pieces, and Mycenaean jewellery. Look for the 4th-century gravestone of Kalliarista and its touching epigram inscribed by her husband, as well as the tiny vases and bowls that formed a child's funerary gifts. Beyond the upper gallery is a sunlit sculpture garden.

The Aphrodite of Rhodes, a more charming version of the eroded 'Marine Venus'

25C2
Argyrokastrou Square, Old Town
0241 75674
Tue–Sun 8:30–3
Cafés in Ermou St (££)
Good
Moderate
Municipal Art Gallery (➤ 28), Archaeological Museum (➤ above), Byzantine Museum (➤ 33)

MOUSEÍO TIS KOSMIKIS TÉCHNIS (MUSEUM OF DECORATIVE ARTS)

The Museum of Decorative Arts is housed in a ground floor room that was once part of the armoury of the Knights of St John. It is more of a folk art museum than its name implies, and has a charming and colourful collection of domestic goods from the 16th to the early 20th century. These include folk costumes from the islands of Sými and Astypalaea, carved and painted chests and bedsteads, carved wall cupboards and other furnishings. There is a large collection of ceramics and fabrics, including carpets and such distinctive items as embroidered bed tents.

An elegant vase from the 6th century BC in the Museum of Ancient Rhodes

MOUSEÍO VIZANTINO (BYZANTINE MUSEUM)

The Byzantine Museum is housed in the splendid Church of Panagia Kastrou, the Virgin of the Castle. This 11th-century building has had a remarkable history. Originally it was the Byzantine Cathedral of Rhodes and had a classic Byzantine 'cross-in-square' form, with a central dome. The church was converted to a Roman Catholic cathedral by the Knights of St John, who replaced the dome with a barrel vault and cross vaults. During the Turkish occupation of Rhodes the building was converted into a mosque complete with minaret, removed during the Italian reconstruction. Today, the church contains a fine collection of Byzantine and post-Byzantine icons and wall-paintings, sculptures and mosaic floors.

- 25C2
- Mouseío Square, Old Town
- Apr–Oct, Tue–Sun 9–3
- Cafés in Ermou (££)
- Few
- Cheap
- Archaeological Museum (➤ 32), Museum of Decorative Arts (➤ 32)

MUSEUM OF ANCIENT RHODES

Located within the Palace of the Grand Masters (➤ 12) this is an outstanding collection of artefacts that leads you through a series of displays from the Stone Age settlement of Rhodes through the classical to the Roman period. Amongst the many exhibits is a fine head of the Sun God Helios, Rhodes' mythic founder. A mosaic floor of the Middle Hellenistic period displays a superb 'New Comedy Mask' that you would swear was a painting rather than an intricate mosaic. Look out for the little bronze figures of bulls and grasshoppers. There are splendid collections of pottery and household goods from all periods displayed in an imaginative way.

- 24B2
- Palace of the Grand Masters, Kleovoulou Square
- 0241 23359; fax 0241 31048
- Apr–Oct, Tue–Sun 8–7, Mon 12–7. Nov–Mar, Tue–Sun 8:30–3
- Café inside Palace (££)
- Few
- Moderate – included in entry fee to Palace
- Ippotón (➤ 15)
- 2,400 Years Exhibition

25C3
Large number of cafés, snack bars/kiosks, restaurants, bars (£–£££)
Few
Mandraki Harbour (➤ 30)

NEW TOWN ✪✪

The New Town is an appealing and cosmopolitan place, a mix of Italian-era art deco and municipal buildings, bland modern hotels, a sprinkling of 1930s mansions, and the shops and offices of the commercial centre. On the Mandraki waterfront, the Italian-built Néa Agorá, the New Market, is a striking feature. Its Ottoman-inspired entrance arch leads to a heptagonal courtyard that is lined with shops, food-kiosks, cafés and tavernas, and has a fish market at its centre. The bustle of the New Market has ebbed in recent years, but there are still plenty of shops and stalls. The exterior perimeter of the building, on Plateía Rimini, has a marvellous selection of delicatessens, bakeries and open-fronted shops selling spices, herbs, nuts, liquor, sweets and Greek specialities. The seafront perimeter is lined with cafés and wickedly indulgent *zaharoplastios* (café-patisseries). Northwest of the market is busy Kiprou Square, the hub of Rhodes's shopping district. The area has numerous fashion salons and general shops that are interspersed with stylish cafés, restaurants and bars. The New Town has pleasant green areas such as the Municipal Park, reached from El Venizelou Street, and the Municipal Gardens, reached from Rimini Square.

Below: *scupture with an exuberant marine theme*
Bottom: *New Town café society*

This famous drum-shaped fountain in the Old Jewish Quarter is decorated with blue tiles depicting shells and sea creatures

OLD JEWISH QUARTER

The Old Jewish Quarter is contained within the most easterly section of Rhodes Old Town, where Jewish merchants and artisans were permitted to live during the Turkish occupation of the island. The focus of the area is Plateía Martyrón Evraión, the Square of the Jewish Martyrs, from where nearly 1500 Rhodian Jews were deported to concentration camps by Nazi forces in 1943. The square is flanked on one side by a handsome building, a 15th-century Archbishop's Palace. A short way along Pindharou to the east, a right turn leads down Dosiadou Street and into Simiou Street, where stands a surviving **synagogue**, itself a reconstruction by the Knights after the original was destroyed during the first Great Turkish seige. Inside there is a superb *hokhláki* (pebble mosaic) floor. Most of the Old Jewish Quarter is a major tourist attraction, its main streets and squares crammed with gift shops, cafés and restaurants. All roads lead to the crowded shopping street of Sokratous, via Ippokrátous Square, notable for its sea horse fountain and the dignified old building of the Kastellania, the medieval stock exchange. Away from the crowds, however, intriguing narrow alleyways lead off the main squares and retain the authentic character of a more everyday Rhodes.

25D2
Rhodes Old Town
Numerous cafés and restaurants (££–£££)
Few
Palace of the Grand Masters (➤ 12), Ippotón (➤ 15), Municipal Baths (➤ 28)

Jewish Synagogue

Dosiadou/Simiou Streets
Daily 10–5 (may be closed during winter months)
Few
Donations welcomed

The Old Town

Distance
1.5km

Time
1 hour

Start point
St Mary's Gate, Commercial Harbour (next gate north of Marine Gate)
25D2

End point
Sokratous
25C2

Lunch
The Walk Inn, Dorieos Square (£)

Church of Ágia Triáda
Tue–Sun 8–2:30

This short walk through the medieval Old Town gives some idea of the pleasure that can be had from seeking out the more remote quarters of this fascinating area.

Go through Pýli Panagías (St Mary's Gate), cross Rodiou, then cross the courtyard of the ruined Church of Our Lady of the City. Keep straight ahead along a paved walkway (Alhadef) fringed with trees. Just before the arch of the Akandia Gate, turn right, up Dionissiou (watch for traffic) and continue along Ekatonos. Pass the ruins of a Roman building, then bear right along the narrow Tlipolemou.

The characteristic narrow alleyways of the old town, with their *hokhláki* (pebble mosaic surfacing), begin to appear.

Keep straight ahead, pass beneath an arch, cross Perikleous, then go under another arch to reach the square of Panagiotu Rodiu and the Church of Ágia Triáda. Pass in front of the church then go left along the twisting and turning Laokoontos to reach a T-junction. Here turn left along Praxitelous, then go right along Kimonous, then left along Klisthenous.

The church of Ágios Georgios in the Old Town

These tiny alleyways are the heart and soul of the Old Town.

At a T-junction turn right along Archbishop Efthymiou and keep round right to reach a square. Turn left along Omirou. After about 100m go right through an arched opening into Dorieos Square.

In the square are the impressive Mosque of Retset Pascha (► 39) with a domed fountain in front of it, and the three-aisled basilica of Ágios Fanoúriou, with restored frescoes.

Leave the square by the far right-hand corner, then turn right along the wonderful Ágios Fanoúriou and follow it to its end to the busy shopping street of Sokratous.

OLD TOWN MOAT

The Old Town Moat was always dry, but was still a formidable barrier to attack. For many years the moat was overgrown and strewn with rubbish, but it is now landscaped and dotted with palm trees and pines and makes a delightful choice for a stroll. There are several entry points to the moat, but a logical approach is through Pyli Petru, the Gate of St Peter, reached from Alexandrias Square at the south end of Mandraki Harbour, and opposite the southern wall of the New Market.The way passes between towering walls and soon reaches a widening of the moat at Exit 1, the handsome Pyli Ambouaz, the d'Amboise Gate. In the bed of the moat lie the remains of a medieval quarry. Lizards scuttle in and out of niches in the moat walls. Soon you come to a central earthwork. Keep to its right. The track leads beneath a bridge, then comes to another earthwork where old stone mortar balls litter the ground like giant hailstones. Keep to the right again. If you go left, you end up in a chilling cul de sac, just as unthinking attackers might have done, only to find themselves with no escape from the threatening parapets above. The track passes beneath another bridge, widens again at the Melina Mercouri Open Air Theatre then exits onto the harbour front road called Prometheus.

- 25C3
- Rhodes Old Town
- New Market and Gate of St Peter (£–££)
- Few
- Medieval Town (► 18)
- Concerts and shows are held at the Melina Mercouri Theatre in summer

Above: *a view of part of the moat and the Old Town Walls*

Vibrantly coloured bougainvillea cascades over the Old Town walls

OLD TOWN WALLS 

Rhodes's Old Town is defined dramatically by its 4km of defensive walls, their silent precincts haunted by the ghosts of bloody siege and ferocious assault. The present walls owe their monumental form to the fortress mentality of the Knights of St John. Major expansion of the walls came in the 1450s as threats of Turkish invasion galvanised the Knights into improving their defences. The first Turkish siege of 1480 was repulsed, but continuing fears of invasion saw even greater expansion of the walls. The dry moat (➤ 37) was deepened and made wider, powerful bastions were erected at strategic points, and island-like earthworks were erected within the moat to create extra defences and to form bottleneck traps for attackers. All of these features survive, partially restored and redesigned in places by the Italians, but generally true to the originals. The walls are still being refurbished today. Walking the walls on organised tours between the Palace of the Grand Masters and the Koskinoú Gate (➤ below) gives an airy view of the stark outer world of siege and defence, as well as marvellous glimpses of the jumbled inner city with its skyline of Byzantine tiled roofs, slender minarets, palm trees and orchards, its dusty backyards and gardens, serpentine alleyways and crumbling walls.

- 24B2
- Only access is on guided walks Tue & Sat 2:45. Tickets from Palace of the Grand Masters, admissions desk
- None
- Moderate
- Palace of the Grand Masters (➤ 12)
- The inner edge and outer openings of the walls are unguarded, so exercise care, especially with children

Late sunlight highlights the Old Town ramparts

OTTOMAN RHODES ✪✪

Moorish buildings on Rhodes have tended to suffer neglect since the Turks were ousted from the island in 1912. However, sporadic refurbishment of Turkish buildings does take place, and the sizeable Muslim population on Rhodes ensures continuing use of several historic mosques. There is no Turkish Quarter as such, but there are a number of splendid old mosques scattered throughout the Old Town. Finest of these is **Tzamí Souleïmán**, erected by the Turkish conqueror of Rhodes in 1522 as a thanksgiving for his triumph. Its rose-red walls and shallow dome dominate the top end of Sokratous. Other notable buildings are **Tzamí Retset Pascha** and the impressive **Tzamí Sultan Mustafá**. At the northern end of the New Town is **Tzamí Tou Mourad Reïs**, located within an engagingly unkempt and tree-shaded Muslim cemetery. The entrance courtyard has *hokhláki* (pebble mosaic) flooring and in one corner stands the little circular mausoleum of Mourad Reïs, a commander of the Turkish navy during the 1522 seige of Rhodes. The cemetery has its own little forest of slender gravestones; the male memorials crowned with turbans, the female memorials, simple blades of stone. There are a number of domed tombs one containing the remains of a Shah of Persia. At the northern end of the graveyard is the Villa Cleobolus, once home to the novelist Lawrence Durrell (➤ 10) but a rather forlorn little building today.

A doorway of the Ottoman period, with embossed decoration and inscriptions

Tzamí Souleïmán
- 24B2
- Sokrátous Square, Old Town
- Not open to public
- Cafés in Orfeos and Sokratous (£–££)

Tzamí Retset Pascha
- 25C2
- Dorieos Square, Old Town
- Not open to public
- Cafés in square (£)

Tzamí Sultan Mustafá
- 25C2
- Aríonos Square, Old Town
- Not open to public
- Cafés in Square (£)
- Municipal Baths (➤ 28)

Tzamí Tou Mourad Reïs
- 24B4
- Koundouriótou Square
- 9–6 (variable)
- Cavalliere, Ioannou Kazouli St (£)
- None
- Free (small donation appreciated if caretaker present)
- Aquarium (➤ 29), Mandraki Harbour (➤ 30)

Around the Island

Beyond Rhodes Town lies a different world which, in the south especially, offers a fascinating contrast to the urban and resort areas. On the west coast there is a thinning out of development once past the airport, and soon this more remote coastline is dominated by the island's forested mountain chain. The east coast is developed as far as Líndos, but beyond there you again encounter an island that seems entirely separate from the busy, popular Rhodes of the brochures. Inland there is yet another world of olive groves and scrub-covered hills that shelter charming villages. You can explore island Rhodes by bus, or more independently by car, and there are good opportunities to walk along remote beaches and in the mountains.

'From the waters of the sea arose an island which is held by the father of the piercing beams of light, the ruler of the steeds whose breath is fire.'

PINDAR
Olympic Ode VII

Left: *the village of Émponas, with Mount Attávyros behind*

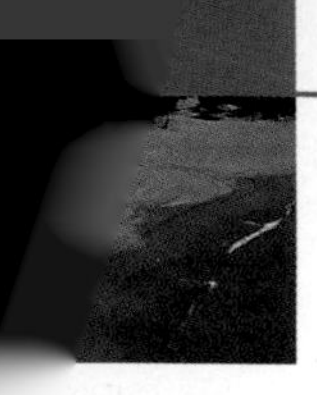

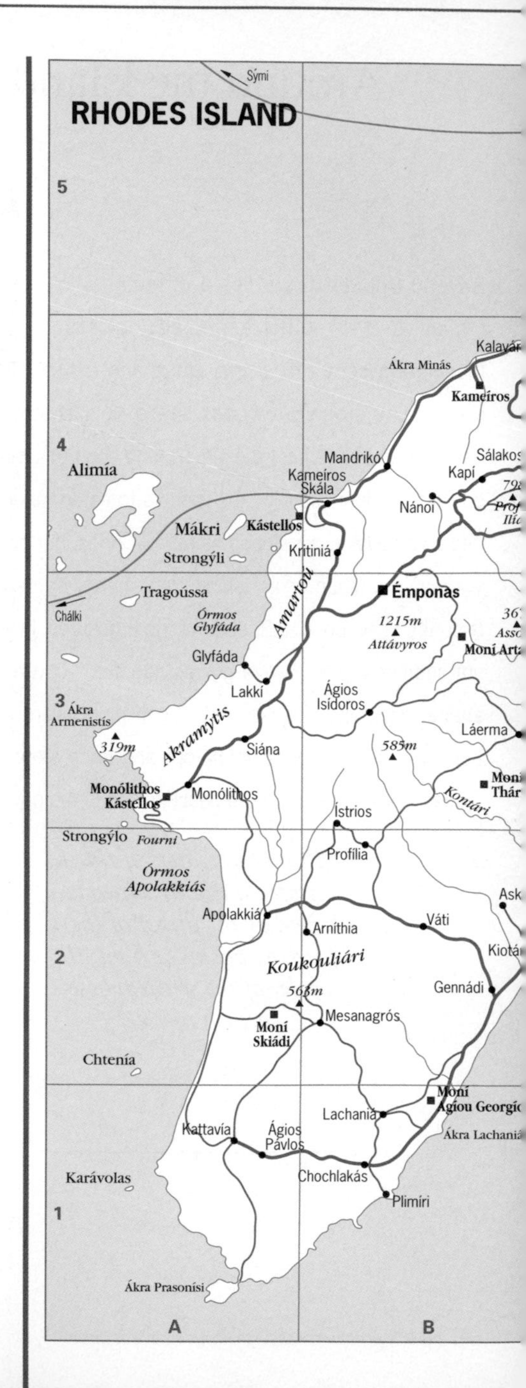
RHODES ISLAND
Sými
Chálki
5
4
3
2
1
A
B
Alimía
Mákri
Kástellos
Strongýli
Tragoússa
Órmos Glyfáda
Amartoú
Glyfáda
Lakkí
Ákra Armenistís
319m
Akramýtis
Siána
Monólithos Kástellos
Monólithos
Strongýlo
Fourni
Órmos Apolakkiás
Apolakkiá
Ákra Minás
Kameíros
Mandrikó
Kameiros Skála
Kritiniá
Nánoi
Kapí
Sálakos
Émponas
1215m
Attávyros
Moní Artá
Ágios Isídoros
Láerma
585m
Kontári
Ístrios
Profília
Arníthia
Váti
Koukouliári
568m
Gennádi
Mesanagrós
Moní Skiádi
Chtenía
Moní Agíou Georgíou
Lachaniá
Ákra Lachaniá
Kattavía
Ágios Pávlos
Chochlakás
Plimíri
Karávolas
Ákra Prasonísi

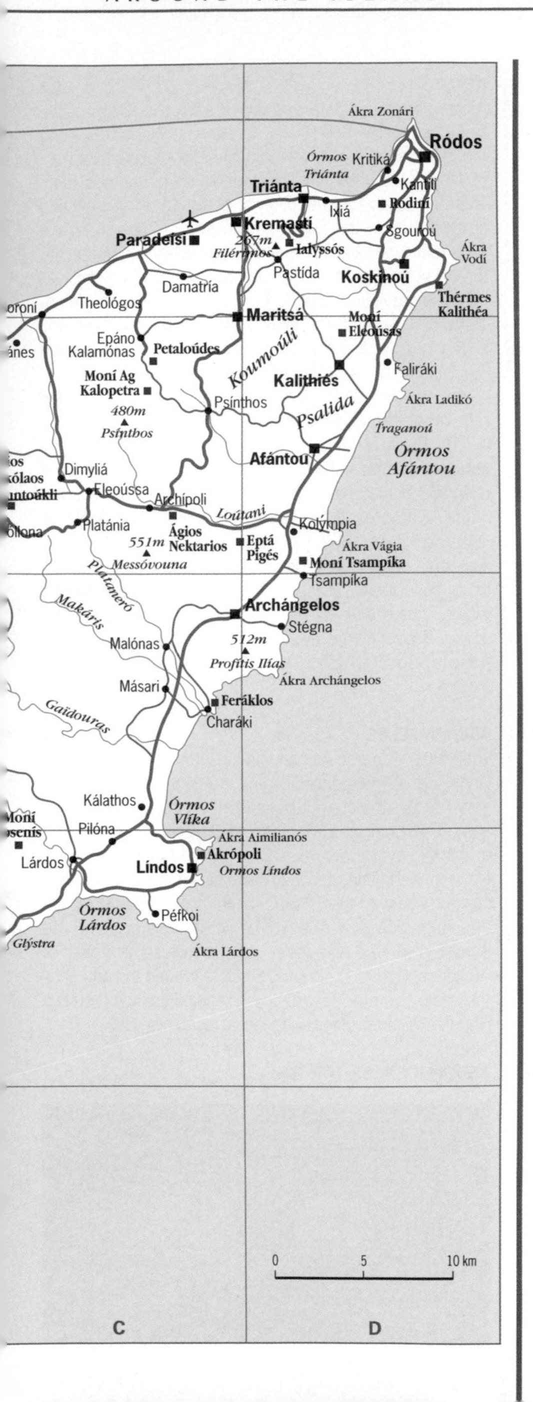
Ákra Zonári
Ródos
Órmos Kritiká
Triánta
Triánta
Kantíli
Rodiní
Ixiá
Kremastí
Paradeísi
Sgouroú
267m
Filérimos
Ialyssós
Ákra Vodí
Pastída
Koskinoú
Damatría
Thérmes Kalithéa
Theológos
Maritsá
Moní Eleoúsas
Epáno Kalamónas
Petaloúdes
Koumoúli
Faliráki
Moní Ag Kalopetra
Kalithiés
Ákra Ladikó
Psínthos
480m
Psalida
Psínthos
Traganoú
Órmos Afántou
Afántou
Dimyliá
Eleoússa
Archípoli
Loútani
Platánia
Kolýmpia
Ágios Nektarios
551m
Eptá Pigés
Ákra Vágia
Messóvouna
Moní Tsampíka
Tsampíka
Plataneró
Archángelos
Makáris
Stégna
512m
Malónas
Profítis Ilías
Ákra Archángelos
Másari
Feráklos
Gaïdouras
Charáki
Kálathos
Órmos Vlíka
Pilóna
Ákra Aimilianós
Akrópoli
Lárdos
Líndos
Órmos Líndos
Órmos Lárdos
Péfkoi
Glýstra
Ákra Lárdos
0
5
10 km
C
D

AFÁNTOU ✪

- 43D4
- East coast, 16km south of Rhodes Town
- Seasonal beach cafés and tavernas (£)
- East side bus, Rodos–Afántou (Rimini Sq)
- Few
- Kolýmpia (➤ 51), Ladikó (➤ 56)
- Pre-Lenten carnival, seventh Sunday before Easter

Afántou beach is entirely detached from the village of the same name. The beach runs for several kilometres along the rather scruffy, but refreshingly undeveloped foreshore of Afántou Bay and is backed by a flanking access road. There is usually room enough to breathe on the sand and shingle even at the height of the season, and there are watersports and beach equipment available in summer. At the north end of the main beach is Traganoú Beach, all white shingle and translucent water in the shelter of Traganoú Headland. The fairly small and compact Traganoú is very popular and there is a military rest and recreation complex here. At the north end of Traganoú Beach, beyond a rocky bluff, is a small beach with caves in the cliff wall of the headland at its far end.

The village of Afántou is a classic example of a coastal community that initially migrated inland to escape the relentless pirate raids of the Byzantine period. The village's name is said to derive from the word for 'hidden' or 'invisible', neatly defining its origins. Today's Afántou is indeed invisible, even from the coast road, and is reached along several link roads that terminate at the attractive village square with its canopied tavernas and cafés. The square is overlooked by Ágios Loukas, the Church of the Assumption, which houses an interesting folklore exhibition.

ARCHÁNGELOS ✪

- 43C3
- East coast, 33km south of Rhodes Town
- Numerous cafés and restaurants (£–££)
- East side bus, Rhodes–Archángelos, daily (Rimini Sq)
- Few
- Charáki (➤ 45), Kolýmpia (➤ 51), Ladikó (➤ 56), Tsampíka (➤ 67), Stégna (➤ 64)
- Mid-Aug, week-long Cultural Festival. 8 Nov, Feast of the Archangels

The large village of Archángelos stands amidst a startling landscape of limestone cliffs and rocky hills. It is a bustling, down to earth place, the centre of an important farming area. The Knights of St John had a castle here and its evocative, overgrown ruins are reached by going halfway along the left-hand branch of the main street. Turn left up a narrow alleyway then keep straight across a little square and go up Sarika Anastasi, following signs for the Acropolis. On the way down, visit the handsome church of Archangel Gabriel Patitiriotis. Clustered round the church is the older, quieter part of the village; quite distinctively Rhodian in its buildings and friendly residents.

ASKLIPEÍO (➤ 13, TOP TEN)

Details of shields on the wall at the Castle of the Knights, Archángelos

CHÁLKI ✪

The small island of Chálki is an elusive place, well out of the mainstream network of inter-island ferries. The island is not a day-trip destination but makes for a pleasant extended stay although not a beach-orientated one; the handful of sand beaches and pebbled coves are crowded in summer. Once dependent on sponge fishing, the island suffered heavy depopulation due to a dramatic decline in the industry during the early 1900s. Today many of the abandoned houses of the port settlement of Niborio have been converted to holiday villas. The virtually uninhabited village of Horió lies 3km inland.

- 42A3 (arrowed from)
- 15km west of Rhodes Island
- Several cafés and tavernas in Niborio
- Few
- Ferry from Kámiros Skála (2:45 departure, but it is advisable to check), returns the next morning. Day excursion possible on Sundays

CHARÁKI ✪✪

The small, custom-built resort of Charáki is pleasantly contained within the gentle crescent of a little bay. There is a shingle and sand beach whose only shortcoming is that it's in full view of a flanking promenade, lined with villas, cafés and tavernas. Charáki stands at the north end of the Bay of Masari and below the ruins of the ancient castle of Feráklos high on its rocky hill. The original Byzantine castle was the first of Rhodes' fortresses to fall to the Knights of St John in 1306, and it became one of the main strongholds on the island until the final Turkish conquest.

You can reach the castle from the north end of Charáki beach by following a concrete road to a water tank, from where rough ground leads up left to a vestigial path to an entrance to the castle's broad inner precincts, now overgrown. Alternatively, a rough track leads from just behind the resort to where a path, then a stone staircase, lead to the entrance. The track continues from this point past several unfinished and abandoned villas to reach the fine sandy beach of Ágia Agáthi, popular, but undeveloped. (A signposted track from the coast road to Ágia Agáthi is best avoided, as it is a long detour and punishing to cars).

- 43C3
- East coast, 40km south of Rhodes Town
- Cafés and tavernas on promenade (£–££)
- East side bus, Rhodes–Charáki, daily (Rimini Sq)
- Few
- Archángelos (► 44), Líndos (► 57)

Above: *Charáki is pleasantly located on a sandy bay, below the castle of Feráklos*

Above: *a carpet weaver in Émponas engaged in producing goods by traditional methods*

ÉMPONAS

- 42B3
- 58km southwest of Rhodes Town
- Several cafés and tavernas (£–££)
- West side bus, Rhodes–Émponas, daily (Averof St)
- Few
- Kritiniá Castle (➤ 54)
- Tours of Emery Winery, Mon–Fri 9–3. Free. ☎ 0246 41208

This large mountain village is the centre of the Rhodian wine trade. Here are located the island's vineyards on terraced fans that spill down from the stark slopes of 1,215m Mt Attávyros. The Emery Winery, at the western outskirts of Émponas, stages conducted tours of its processing plant and caters for numerous coach parties. The village does a strong secondary trade in carpet weaving, embroidery and general souvenirs. Take a stroll in the upper reaches of Émponas, where there are a number of venerable carpet weavers at work, especially near the Church of Panayia.

EPTÁ PIGÉS (THE SEVEN SPRINGS)

- 43C4
- East coast, 30km south of Rhodes Town
- Open access
- Seasonal taverna beside car park (££)
- East side bus, Rhodes–Kolýmpia, daily (Rimini Sq)
- Free
- Kolýmpia (➤ 51)

The pleasant, sun-dappled enclave of Eptá Pigés was created by the Italians in the 1920s to supply water for irrigating the coastal colony of Kolýmpia. The eponymous Seven Springs are hidden somewhere amidst deep woodland. A narrow aqueduct-tunnel, 186m long, siphons off water from just below the site car park to a pretty lake and waterfall hidden amidst the trees. Most guide books invite you to splash your way through this nightmare, but it is better to stay in the open air by walking directly uphill from the tunnel entrance to reach the access road and the halfway escape shaft. Cross the road and follow a landscaped path opposite (unsigned) to the holding dam where the tunnel disburses its water. The artificial lake is deep, non-potable and definitely not for diving into.

DID YOU KNOW?

The name Profítis Ilías reflects the Greek custom of naming mountains after the prophet Elijah (Ilías), who is said to have ascended to heaven from a mountain top.

Through the Pines of Profítis Ilías

This delightful walk follows the landscaped tracks and stone staircases on the wooded summit of Profítis Ilías mountain (► 22).

From the junction below the kafenío *(café), follow the rough road to the right, signed Childrens' Camp and Athletic Centre. After about 400m, look for rocky steps rising through the trees on the right. Leave the road and follow the steps uphill.*

The stone staircases of Profítis Ilías were constructed in the 1920s by the Italians as part of a landscaping scheme.

Where the path fades near a higher bend in the road, bear round right and uphill. Pass beneath a single power cable and then another cable slung between trees. Pick up the stepped path just beyond this second cable. Follow a mix of broken steps and stone-lined path uphill and over a flat area studded with rocks, then descend gently to reach a junction of paths.

Up to the left is the summit of Profítis Ilías, crammed with radio masts and out of bounds to the public.

Turn right at the junction. Descend wooded slopes, then at a junction by two rocks go left, passing above an old concrete water tank. Scramble round some fallen rocks, then continue winding downhill. Pass a derelict building, then bear right and descend through zig-zags. Pass above the kafenío.

On top of a small cliff on the left is the now derelict villa built for Mussolini. You can reach the building and the church beyond it by diverting up a stone staircase on the left.

On the main route, turn right and down steps to the road, then turn right to reach the kafenío.

Distance
5km

Time
2 hours

Start/end point
Profítis Ilías *kafenío*
42B4

Lunch
Profítis Ilías *kafenío* (£)

The sun-dappled stone stairways offer a gentle ascent through the shady pine trees at Profítis Ilías

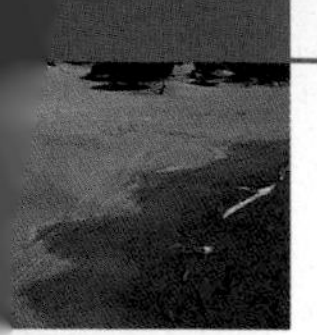

- 43D4
- East coast, 15km south of Rhodes Town
- Huge range of cafés, bars and restaurants (£–£££)
- East side bus, Rhodes–Faliráki–Kalithies, daily (Rimini Sq)
- Good
- Thérmes Kalithéa (➤ 66), Ladikó (➤ 56)

FALIRÁKI

Rhodes's major beach resort of Faliráki is focused entirely on tourism, all of which is based on the sweep of sand that lines the long foreshore. The palatial hotels at the north end cater for a more restrained clientele than the youthful crowds who frequent the main resort, where every kind of watersport is available – including parascending, banana boat rides, waterskiing and jetskiing – and bungee jumping. Faliráki is bursting at the seams with bars, cafés, restaurants, discos and nightclubs, although the peripheral hotels are outside the reverberation zone.

- 42B2
- Southeast coast, 77km south of Rhodes Town
- Several cafés and tavernas in village and behind beach (£–££)
- East side bus, Rhodes–Kattavía, Tue–Thu, Sat (Rimini Sq)
- Few
- Asklipeío (➤ 13)

Above: *the bustling resort of Faliráki, once a small fishing village*

GENNÁDI

The village of Gennádi is the last sizeable settlement before the remoter reaches of the far south. Gennádi is an unassuming village with a great deal of charm, and its villagers enhance this with their engaging friendliness. Located on the rising ground above the coast road, the village is a pleasing jumble of white-painted houses traversed by long narrow streets. In the northwest area is the Church of Ágios Ioannis, located within a complex of old buildings that surrounds a *hokhláki* (pebble mosaic floored) courtyard with a central cypress tree. On the way to the church is a beautifully refurbished olive-pressing barn, complete with equipment. Gennádi's beach is a very long stretch of sand and gravel, which shelves away a short distance offshore.

GLYSTRA ✪✪

The sandy crescent of Glystra beach is a surprising treat amidst a coastline of barren rock, alongside the undeveloped stretch of road south of Lárdos. It is not empty, however, as it is very accessible and irresistible to anyone driving by. The sand is clean and silky and the beach is backed by tree-studded dunes. South of Glystra, the rocky shoreline can be reached from the roadside in several places, but be careful of loose rock and shale when you are descending.

- 43C2
- East coast, 69km south of Rhodes Town
- Seasonal snack bar (£)
- East side bus, Rhodes–Asklipio, daily; Rhodes–Kattavía, Tue–Thu, Sat (Rimini Sq)
- None (beach is accessible from the level)
- Asklipeío (➤ 13), Lárdos (➤ 56)

IALYSSÓS (➤ 14, TOP TEN)

IXIÁ ✪

The first tourist beach south of Rhodes Town on the west coast, Ixiá has been long established as a resort, though its identity is all but overpowered by the dense surroundings of huge luxury hotels. Every kind of watersport is available on the long, narrow sand and shingle beach. You may feel trapped betwen the busy coast road and the offshore flight path to Rhodes airport, but if close-quarters sociability and convenience appeals, then Ixiá has enough and to spare.

- 43D5
- West coast, 5km southwest of Rhodes Town
- Large number of cafés, bars, tavernas and restaurants (£–££)
- West side bus, Rhodes–Paradissi, daily (Averof St)
- Few
- Monte Smith (➤ 31), Ialyssós (➤ 14)

KAMEÍROS (➤ 16, TOP TEN)

Above: *Glystra's beach has some of the finest sand on the island*

Left: *blue-painted fishing boats match the still blue ocean at Ixiá*

The bell tower of the Church of St Paraskevi at Kattavía

KATTAVÍA

- 42A1
- Southwest coast, 96km south of Rhodes Town
- Restaurant Penelope (££)
- East side bus, Rhodes–Kattavía, Tue–Thu, Sat (Rimini Sq)
- Few
- Plimíri (➤ 61), Prasonísi (➤ 61)

When you reach Kattavía, you feel as if you have truly escaped from the rest of Rhodes. This is no historical backwater, though, as there has been a settlement here from ancient times (remains from the Mycenean period have been found). The Italians left their inevitable mark in the shape of model farms amid the wheat fields of the area. Just before reaching the village you pass the derelict Italian-era farm of Ágios Pavlos with its church tower of San Paolo. The central crossroads in Kattavía has several cafés and tavernas and in the Byzantine church of the Dormition of the Virgin there are fine 17th-century frescoes. The Church of St Paraskevi has a flamboyant and vividly coloured bell tower.

KIOTÁRI

- 42B2
- East coast, 62km south of Rhodes Town
- Tavernas (£-££) on beach road
- East side bus, Rhodes–Kiotári, daily (Rimini Sq)
- Few
- Asklipeío (➤ 13)

The beach resort of Kiotári was once the coastal settlement of Asklipeío before the community moved inland during the Byzantine period to escape repeated pirate raids. Today Kiotári is given over entirely to tourism. The northern section of the beach has the most character. A tiny cane-built hut still crowns the small rock promontory of Hilioravdi, the Rock of One Thousand Stakes – a reference to a medieval incident during which local people sowed the beach with sharpened stakes as a defence against pirate landings. The hut was built by a local school-teacher and his pupils over fifty years ago.

KOLÝMPIA

The resort of Kolýmpia is famed for its long approach avenue, lined by towering eucalyptus trees. The Italians built model farms throughout the coastal plain here during the early 20th century; the planting of the trees was part of a drainage scheme. At the avenue's seaward end it branches; the left branch leads quickly to the small North Beach that is the southern termination of the sweeping Afántou beach. The right-hand branch takes you to a rather barren area of partially excavated sand. There is a small beach here and a harbour sheltering fishing boats. A short distance further on from here is the larger and more appealing South Beach.

- 43D4
- East coast, 21km south of Rhodes Town
- Taverna and cafés overlook both beaches (£–££)
- East side bus, Rhodes–Kolýmpia, daily (Rimini Sq)
- Few
- Afántou (► 44), Archángelos (► 44), Eptá Pigés (► 46), Stégna (► 64)

Left: *the 3km avenue of trees to the beach* Below: *the church at Kremastí, with its geometric lawns*

KREMASTÍ

Kremastí is one of Rhodes' larger villages, where you can capture the mood of everyday Rhodian life in cafés and tavernas. The main focus of the village is the handsome Church of the Panagia, Our Lady of Kremastí, a large building within a complex of mature trees and formal lawns and with a flanking arcade surfaced with superb *hokhláki* (pebble mosaic) flooring. The interior walls are covered in modern icons; there is a splendid golden iconostasis, or altar screen, and extravagant chandeliers. Adjacent to the church is a bone-white classical building that houses a library. This building and the church were funded by donations from expatriate local people, mainly living in America.

- 43C5
- West coast, 13km southwest of Rhodes Town
- Several tavernas and cafés in main street (£)
- West side bus, Rhodes–Kremastí, daily (Averof St)
- Few
- Ialyssós (► 14)
- Please dress soberly in the church; no photography inside

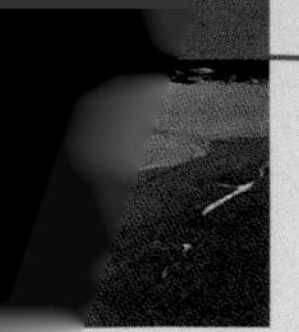

In the Know

If you only have a short time to visit Rhodes and would like to get a real flavour of the island, here are some ideas:

10 Ways to Be a Local

Go shopping in Rhodes New Town and treat yourself to something with a designer label.
Resist the beach and head inland to explore the mountain villages.
Wear dark glasses all the time.
Drink *Ellinikós kafés* (Greek coffee) slowly with an accompanying glass of *neró* (water).
Join a local carnival in earnest by dressing up.
Search out Greek specialities in the food shops round the New Market in Rhodes Town. Be ready to sample anything.
Attend a musical or drama performance at the Municipal Theatre in Rhodes Town. Even if you cannot understand Greek the performances are enjoyable.
Learn some greetings and courtesies in Greek.
Dress soberly in churches – make a donation and light a candle, whatever your beliefs are.
Reciprocate the friendliness and warmth of the islanders.

10 Good Places to Have Lunch

Agapitos Taverna (£) ✉ Asklipeío ☎ 0244 47255. Welcoming owners at this village taverna where you can enjoy typical Rhodian cooking.
Althaimeni (££) ✉ Kameíros Skala ☎ 0246 31303. If fish is your favourite then this is the place. Also serves meat and vegetable dishes on a pleasant terrace overlooking the harbour.
Cavalliere (£) ✉ Ioannou Kazouli St, Rhodes New Town ☎ 0241 22932. Café-patisserie that offers pizzas and other snacks with a great selection of pastries.
Cristos Corner (£) ✉ Monólithos ☎ 0246 61310. Friendly country taverna with a range of grilled food and snacks.
Fashion House Café (£) ✉ 46b Amerikis St, Rhodes New Town ☎ 0241 78369. Tasty snacks and big range of hot and cold drinks from coffee to beers, wines and spirits.
Hatzikelis (££) ✉ 9 Solomou Alhadef St, Rhodes Old Town ☎ 0241 27215. Excellent fish dishes, good selection of *mezdéhes* (starters) and meat dishes in this classic Old Town eaterie.
Mike's Taverna (£) ✉ Off Aríonos Square, Rhodes Old Town. Friendly, laid-back style in this taverna where you might even be serenaded with guitar playing.
Stani Pool Café (£) ✉ Shopping Centre, Rodosland, Iraklidon St, Ialyssós ☎ 0241 96422. Lunch break by the pool at this pleasant café-bar that specialises in snacks and mouthwatering pastries, sweets and ice-cream.
To Limanaki (£) ✉ Kolýmpia ☎ 0241 56240. Range of snacks and meals at this long-established taverna overlooking the beach.
Yiannis Restaurant-Taverna (£) ✉ 41 Platonas St, off Sokratous St, Rhodes Old Town ☎ 0241 36535. No-frills taverna, but with excellent food and drink and outstanding value.

10 Mementoes of Rhodes

- Lace and ceramics from Líndos
- *Souma* spirit from Siána
- Mountain honey from Monólithos or Siána
- A carpet or rug from Émponas
- Wine from the Caer or Emery wineries; or try an independent winery such

Genuine hand-made lace from Líndos is worth its expensive price tag

as Anastasia Triantafillou near Petaloúdes
- Gold or silver jewellery
- A hand-painted icon
- *Kataifi* (honey cake) and *baklava* (syrup cake)
- Leather goods from Archángelos
- Olive wood bowls and utensils

10 Best Beaches

Afántou for lots of space (► 44)
Charáki for the convenience of the beachside promenade, or nearby Ágia Agáthi for simplicity and for excellent sand (► 45)
Fourni for a sense of really being away from the rest of Rhodes and for the spectacular backdrop of forested mountains (► 20)
Glystra for superb sand, shallow water and absence of development (► 49)
Péfkoi for a selection of small beaches with good sand (► 60)
Plimíri for remoteness and space (► 61)
Prasonísi for wide open spaces and a choice of spots for windsurfing or sunbathing (► 61)
Traganoú for clear water and white shingle (► 44)
Tsampíka for absence of beachside development and wild surroundings (► 67)
Vlíka for a sense of luxury and good facilities (► 67)

10 Best Viewpoints

- Feráklos castle, Charáki (► 45)
- Ialyssós, from the fortress and cross (► 14)
- Kritiniá castle (► 54)
- Líndos Acropolis (► 17)
- Monte Smith (► 31)
- Monólithos castle (► 20)
- Old Town walls, Rhodes (► 38)
- Profítis Ilías ridge (► 22)
- Rolói, the Turkish clock tower, Old Town
- Tsampíka monastery (► 66)

The beach at Ágia Agáthi, one of Rhodes's best; a 25-minute walk from Charáki

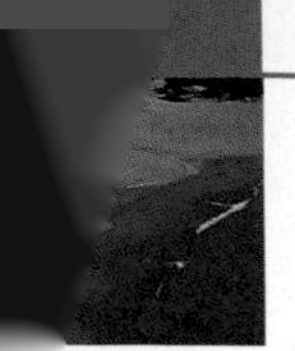

KRITINÍA CASTLE

- 42B4
- West coast, 34km southwest of Rhodes Town
- Castle open access, museum variable
- Café/taverna at Kritinía (£), snack bar at museum (£)
- West side bus, Rhodes–Kritinía, daily (Averof St)
- None at castle. Few at Kritinía
- Émponas (➤ 46)

The ruins of the medieval *kastello* of Kritinía stand on top of a 131m hill overlooking olive groves and pine woods above the sea. This was one of the key strategic fortresses of the Knights of St John and the walls once boasted the coats of arms of several Grand Masters. Today the castle is a lonely ruin that rises through several levels to a final vantage point offering outstanding views. About 3km southeast of the castle is the quiet little village of Kritinía. On the main road above the village is the Kritiniá Folklore Museum, which contains an interesting collection of rural artefacts, crafts and traditional dress.

LACHANIÁ

- 42B1
- East coast, 88km south of Rhodes Town
- Several tavernas/cafés on the upper approach road (£). Taverna in village square (£)
- East side bus, Rhodes–Kattavía, Tue–Thu, Sat (Rimini Sq)
- Few
- Plimíri (➤ 61)

Hidden amidst deep green countryside, the peaceful village of Lachaniá is another of those remote settlements whose origins may date as far back as the Bronze Age. Many of Lachaniá's delightful 19th-century houses have been imaginatively restored. Wander down through the village from the upper approach road to reach the tiny square. Its solitary taverna and detached church tower are overshadowed by an enormous plane tree. Two fountains add a refreshing murmur to the square; one has a surviving Moorish inscription. Just up from the square, following the left-hand exit, stands the ruin of an old mill, windowless and doorless. It is propped firmly with wooden braces and should not be entered, but the huge mill wheel is clearly visible from outside.

Outstanding views of the coast from Kritiniá Castle

A Drive Around Northern Rhodes

This route illustrates the enjoyable contrast between the holiday coasts of northern Rhodes and the island's mountainous interior.

Leave Rhodes Town by the west coast road and pass through Ixiá, Ialyssós and Kremastí. After 27km you reach Kalavárda and turn left, signed Sálakos and Émponas. Climb steadily to Sálakos then continue below the craggy, pine-clad slopes of Profítas Ilías (➤ 22). Just past the village of Kapí, at a junction by a tiny church, go left, signed Profítas Ilías and Eleoússa. Follow the twisting road uphill to reach the settlement of Profítas Ilías.

Distance
93km

Time
6–8 hours, depending on diversions to beaches

Start/end point
Rhodes Town
43D5

Lunch
Profítis Ilías *kafenío* (£)

Below the roadside *kafenío* (café) is an Italian-era hotel and the Church of Profítis Ilías.

Leave Profítas Ilías by keeping straight ahead at the junction just beyond the café. Follow occasional signs for Archípoli and Eleoússa. Watch out for some nasty potholes. Pass the wayside church of Ágios Nikólaos Fountoúkli and continue to Eleoússa.

The art deco fountain and pool at the entrance to Eleoússa

Eleoússa was colonised by Italians in the early 20th century and their legacy is a huge art deco fountain at the village entrance, a square of decaying Italianate buildings, and a church.

Turn immediately right at the square, pass in front of the church steps, then go left at the junction and follow signs to reach Archípoli. Continue to the east coast road, passing on the way the monastery church of Ágios Nektarios and the the entrance road to Eptá Pigés (➤ 46). At the coast road, turn left for Rhodes Town.

You can divert to Kolýmpia (➤ 51) or Afántou (➤ 44) beaches for a late dip on the way.

- 43D4
- East coast, 17km south of Rhodes Town
- Tavernas/cafés at both beaches (£)
- East side bus, Rhodes–Afántou (Rimini Sq). 1.4km walk from coast road junction
- Few
- Afántou (➤ 44), Archángelos (➤ 44), Faliráki (➤ 48)

Ladikó – unspoilt beaches and good cliff-top walks

LADIKÓ ✪✪

Known locally as Anthony Quinn Bay, this attractive area of coastline to the south of Faliráki incorporates two small rock coves with tiny beaches. They are well known and popular but there is minimal development, thus adding to the appeal of crystal clear water and vegetated headlands, dense with wild shrubs and flowers. The small bay to the south (the first one reached along the approach from the main road) has a small sandy beach. The Anthony Quinn connection relates to the filming of parts of *The Guns of Navarone* that took place in the northerly bay, where there is a rocky foreshore and picturesque cliffs. A pleasant cliff path runs north from here and, inland about 1km, leads to the scrubby headland of Cape Ladikó, which overlooks Faliráki's southern beach.

- 43C2
- East coast, 55km south of Rhodes Town
- Tavernas, cafés, bars at central junction
- East side bus, Rhodes–Lárdos (Rimini Sq)
- Few
- Glystra (➤ 49), Líndos (➤ 57), Pefka (➤ 60)
- Please dress soberly in the church; no photography inside

LÁRDOS ✪

The inland village of Lárdos has a busy commercial life, but it still caters for holidaymakers, and there are lots of tavernas, cafés and music bars clustered round its broad central junction. At the centre of the junction is an art deco fountain, a legacy of the Italian era. The village has an excellent fish market and a number of useful shops. The Church of Ágios Taxiarchas is tucked away in the older part of the village and is an impressive building with a big bell tower and tall cypress trees crowding its entrance courtyard. Every building in the old village seems to have a lemon tree in its garden, and there are some vividly painted doors and doorcases. Lárdos beach is about 2km south and is fairly mundane, but undeveloped.

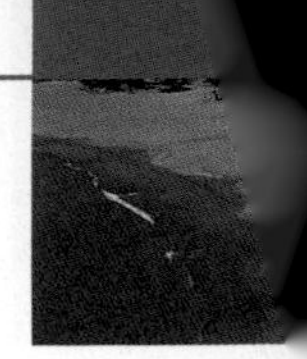

Líndos

Líndos is an impossibly picturesque village; a labyrinth of white-painted Dodecanesian-style houses climbing the slopes to the dramatic Acropolis and Knights' castle. The village is, of course, a hugely popular visitor attraction, and from Easter onwards it is crowded by day and fairly lively by night. The Acropolis (➤ 17) is the main attraction, but Líndos has much more to offer than this splendid monument. Its narrow streets are empty of traffic and locals carry everything in motorbike trailers with which they negotiate some alarming challenges amidst the steeper streets. In some ways Líndos is robbed of its inherent character by the sheer pressure of visitors and by the 'guided tour' atmosphere that dominates proceedings – in several languages. Yet the village is still captivating, especially if you allow time to wander and seek out less well-known ancient ruins, the tiny churches, and the quieter corners.

Ancient Líndos was the most prestigious of the three great city-states of Rhodes, the others being Kameíros (➤ 16) and Ialyssós (➤ 14). When the three cities combined to found the unified city of Rhodes, Líndos continued to prosper; its sanctuary of Lindian Athena remained a place of pilgrimage until Roman times. The Knights of St John kept a strong presence here, and during the Turkish era, Líndos was a prosperous seagoing community. Modern Líndos still recalls this history of commerce and culture.

43C2

East coast, 56km south of Rhodes Town

Numerous cafés, taverna-bars and restaurants (££–£££)

East side bus, Rhodes–Líndos (Rimini Sq)

Charáki (➤ 45), Péfkoi (➤ 60), Moní Thari (➤ 60), Vlíka (➤ 67)

Municipal Tourist Office, Main Square ☎ 0244 31900. Open all day in summer

Líndos, an entrancing jumble of white-painted houses

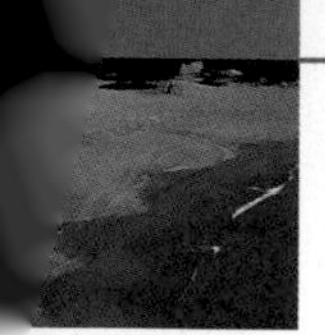

What to See in Líndos

ACROPOLIS (➤ 17, TOP TEN)

ANCIENT SITES

The prime site of the Acropolis apart, there are a number of other ancient sites scattered throughout the Líndos area. Within the village itself is the well-preserved 4th-century BC amphitheatre. It is located on the south-western side of the Acropolis just below the Stavri Square car park. Near by are the remains of a large building, thought to have been a temple of the 3rd or 2nd century BC. Later Christian churches were built over the site. Directly opposite the Acropolis, on the side of Krana Hill and above the highest houses of the village, is the ruin of a monumental necropolis, the tomb of a wealthy Hellenistic family. On Cape Ágios Emilianos, across the main bay from the Acropolis, is the so-called 'Tomb of Kleoboulos', a large circular mausoleum composed of stone slabs. It can be reached by a path from the main beach. There is no convincing evidence that this is the tomb of Kleoboulos, a famous ruler of Líndos.

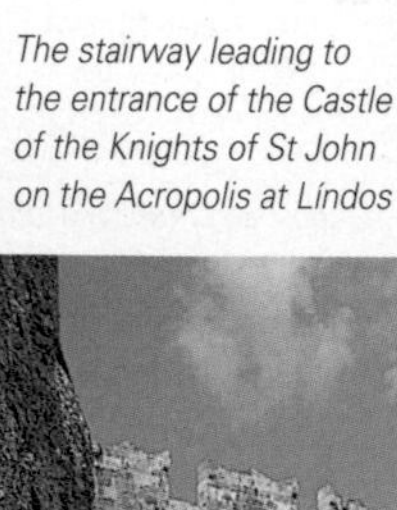

The stairway leading to the entrance of the Castle of the Knights of St John on the Acropolis at Líndos

BEACHES

On the north side of the village is a substantial bay in the shelter of the Acropolis hill. Directly below the Acropolis lies a small harbour where fishing boats moor. Further round the bay is Líndos's very busy main beach. There are several tavernas and bars, beach furniture can be hired and water sports are available. There is another beach further round the bay, and bathing places beyond the headland of Cape Ágios Emilianos. To the south of the Acropolis lies the

remarkable natural harbour of St Paul, where the evangelist is said to have landed on his mission to spread Christianity.

HOUSES OF THE CAPTAINS ✪

An earthquake of 1610 devastated Líndos but the settlement was rebuilt in traditional style, and today's houses, a mix of simple vernacular buildings and handsome Gothic mansions, enhanced with subtle Byzantine and Moorish features, stand behind their high walls and inner courtyards where there is much use made of the exquisite pebble flooring called *hokhláki*. The Líndian doorways, called *pyliónes*, often have fine carving on their doorcases and pediments. Wealth from seagoing enriched Líndos, and many of the finer houses were built by sea captains. Several of these restored captains' houses are open for public viewing, although they are often tied in with restaurants or gift shops. You can get details from the tourist office.

PANAGÍA (CHURCH OF THE ASSUMPTION OF OUR LADY) ✪✪

Panagía is the main church of Líndos and stands at the heart of the village. It dates from medieval times but has been lovingly cared for and refurbished over the years. The characteristic exterior is rather engulfed by its close-knit surroundings but the interior is overwhelming, a superb example of Orthodox decoration. Late 19th-century frescoes, restored in the 1920s, cover the walls and depict vivid biblical scenes. There are numerous fine icons, and the wooden altar screen and Bishop's throne are beautifully carved. The pebble mosaic floor is outstanding. There is a strict requirement for visitors to dress soberly, and photography is not allowed.

Top: *the main beach at Líndos, seen from the approach to the Acropolis*
Above: *elegant Líndian architecture at the heart of the village*

> **DID YOU KNOW?**
>
> Líndos was ruled during the 6th century BC by the peaceful 'Tyrant' Kleoboulos. In Ancient Greece, the title of Tyrant, or *turannos*, signified an absolute ruler, but had no connotations of cruelty or of modern 'tyranny'. Kleoboulos was considered a man of great moderation and wisdom.

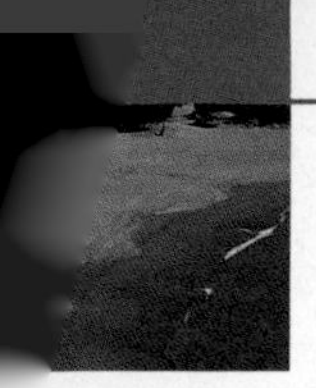

Right: *the small domed monastery of Moní Thari*
Below: *Péfkoi is popular with both visitors and locals*

- 42B3
- East coast, 84km southwest of Rhodes Town
- Small snack bar at entrance (£)
- East side bus, Rhodes–Láerma (Rimini Sq)
- Good (access ramp)
- Líndos (➤ 57), Péfkoi (➤ below)
- Please dress soberly if visiting the monastery – smocks are provided for anyone in shorts or brief tops. No photography inside

MONÍ THARI

Deep inland at the centre of Rhodes lies the monastery of the Archangel Michael at Thari. It is reached from the pleasant village of Láerma. You follow the road through Láerma and after about 50m keep left at an unsignposted junction. Continue along an unsurfaced, but reasonable track, for about 4km through pleasantly wooded countryside, following signs to the monastery. Moní Thari is said to be the oldest religious foundation on the island and ruins within the grounds date from the 9th century. Today's monastery is run on thoroughly modern lines, however, and it even has its own television channel and a triple belfry with seven electronically operated bells. Inside the handsome Byzantine church, traditional Orthodoxy is vividly expressed through the splendid frescoes and carved wooden altar piece.

MONÓLITHOS (➤ 20, TOP TEN)

- 43C2
- East coast, 60km south of Rhodes Town
- Cafés and tavernas on approach road to beach (£)
- East side bus, Rhodes–Péfkoi (Rimini Sq)
- Few
- Lárdos (➤ 56), Líndos (➤ 57), Moní Thari (➤ above)

PÉFKOI

In many ways the beach resort of Péfkoi has become a dormitory suburb of Líndos. The resort developed where only olive groves and a few fishermen's houses once stood. There are now numerous villas and small hotels with attendant tavernas, bars and shops. Most are low key and Péfkoi is fairly quiet, relative to Rhodes's more frenetic resorts. There is a string of pleasant, sandy beaches along the curve of the sheltered bay on which Péfkoi stands.

PETALOÚDES (➤ 21, TOP TEN)

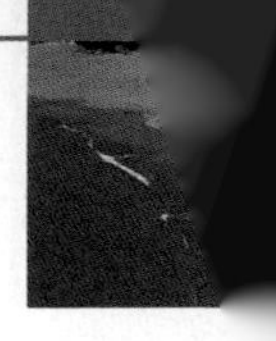

Looking out to sea from inside the monastery courtyard at Plimíri

PLIMÍRI ✪✪

You need to make an effort to reach this fine beach in the far south of Rhodes, but the chance of having some space to yourself is the reward. The absence of permanent development is another bonus and the only activity is at the concrete quay where fishing boats moor overnight. Plimíri's beach runs in a long elegant curve and fringes a shallow bay between the fishing quay and the narrow Cape Germata in the south. At the north end of the beach is the rather stark white building of the Monastery of Zoodohos Pigi ('Source of Life'), an intriguing structure that dates from the 1840s and is built over the ruins of an early Christian church. Incorporated into the exterior of the monastery are classical columns with Corinthian capitals.

- 42B1
- East coast, 90km south of Rhodes Town
- Seasonal taverna (£)
- Few
- Kattavía (➤ 50), Lachaniá (➤ 54)

PRASONÍSI ✪

The lonely cape of Akra Praso lies at the most southerly point of Rhodes on the hilly promontory of Prasonísi. The cape is connected to the mainland by a broad sand bar that is awash during the winter months when there is a rise in sea level and when wind-driven swells roll across the bar. In summer the sand bar is exposed and creates a choice of beach venues to either side; fresh and breezy for windsurfing on the northwest shore, quieter waters for sunbathing on the eastern side. The mainland beach at Prasonísi is enormous, a vast, flat expanse of hard-packed sand, with softer sand along the water's edge. Development is increasing, but the beach is big enough to cope with it.

- 42A1
- South coast, 105km southwest of Rhodes Town
- Restaurants and café-bars at entrance to beach (£)
- East side bus, Rhodes–Prasonísi (Rimini Sq), seasonal service
- Few
- Kattavía (➤ 50)

Food & Drink

The reputation of Greek food and drink has languished, unfairly, in the shadow of French and Italian cuisine and wine-making. The best Greek tavernas represent the highest standards of traditional cooking, and a modern approach to Greek cuisine is found in many top restaurants, while Rhodes produces some of the best wines in the Mediterranean.

A light, refreshing meal of Greek salad with feta cheese and a glass of wine

Mezédhes (starters)

Making a meal of it in a Greek taverna may mean that you never get past the *mezédhes*. The Greek style of eating *mezédhes* is to order half a dozen mixed plates and then for everyone to dig in. A Greek salad (*horiatiki*) is a good way to start any meal or is just right for a light lunch. The best *horiatiki* are plentiful and comprise a marvellous mix of green salad with cucumber, tomatoes and onions, the whole capped with a generous slice of feta cheese sprinkled with herbs. *Mezédhes* worth trying include *manitaria* (mushrooms), *keftedes* (spicy meatballs), *dolmadakia* (rice wrapped in vine leaves), *potopoulo* (chicken portions), *saganáki* (fried cheese), *oktapóthis* (octopus), *spanokeftedes* (spinach balls) and *bourekakia* (meat pies). Add to all this a couple of dips such as *tzatziki* (garlic and cucumber yoghurt) or *melitzanosalata* (aubergine and garlic).

Meat Dishes

Meat dishes on Rhodes follow the Greek standards of moussaka, *souvlaki* (shish kebab with meat, peppers, onions and tomatoes), *pastitsio* (lamb or goat meat with macaroni and tomatoes), *stifádo* (beef stew with tomato sauce and onions) and *padakia* (grilled lamb or goat chops). *Souvlaki* is a good standby, but you might be better settling for chicken (*kotópoulo*) *souvlaki*, because veal or pork on the grill can be tough in some tavernas. Lamb *souvlaki* is usually good but not easily found. Any meat dish that is braised or stewed is usually good.

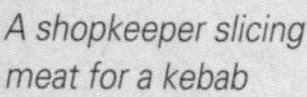

A shopkeeper slicing meat for a kebab

Fish

Rhodes has always been noted for its fish and the island boasts some outstanding *psarotavernas* (fish restaurants). But overfishing, pollution and a general rise in prices has meant that while the choice is still good, fish dishes can often be very expensive. It is also difficult to know whether fish on offer is locally caught or is imported, frozen or farmed versions. Reasonably priced dishes include *marides* (whitebait deep-fried in olive oil and sprinkled with lemon), and swordfish, either in meaty steaks or as *xsifhia,* chunks on a kebab. *Kalamarákia* (fried baby squid) is another favourite. Red mullet and lobster tend to be more expensive.

Drink

Rhodian wines have a good reputation and provided you are not a wine snob, you will enjoy some excellent vintages from the major island wine producers CAER and Emery Wineries, the latter based at Émponas (➤ 46). CAER labels worth trying include Ilios, a dry white wine produced from the Athiri grape, and the Moulin range of white, rosé and red wine. Good Emery wines include the Cava red and first-class Chablis-style Villare dry white. Distinctive wines from smaller Rhodian wineries, such as the Anastasia Triantafillou Winery (➤ 83), are available in some island restaurants. Most tavernas have their own house wine, which can often be reasonable. Retsina, resinated white wine, is an acquired taste and can sometimes scar the palate. Kourtaki is a decent retsina to try. Light beers and lagers, such as Amstel and the Greek Mythos, are available generally.

A chef proudly displays an appetising platter of assorted seafood garnished with salad

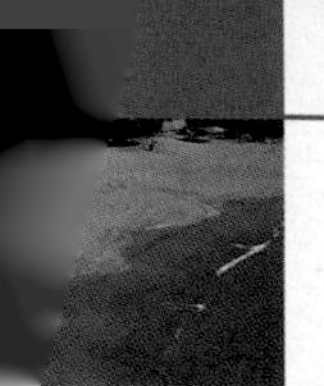

PROFÍTIS ILÍAS (➤ 22, TOP TEN)

SIÁNA

The village of Siána stands on the south-facing side of the 823m-high Mt Akramytis, below forested slopes from which limestone cliffs soar into the sky. Siána is famed for its exquisite honey and its grape distillate, *soumá*. Siána honey has a distinctive flavour, imparted by the herbs and mountain flowers on which the bees feed. Production of *soumá* is prohibited throughout Greece, but Siána benefits from an Italian-era licence that is still extant, allowing the villagers to sell this powerful drink. The impressive single-aisled Church of Ágios Pandeliemon lies at the heart of the village just below the main road. There is good walking to be had in the area, but venturing onto the higher reaches of Mt Akramytis requires experience in hill walking and rock scrambling.

- 42A3
- West coast, 50km southwest of Rhodes Town
- Cafés and tavernas in main street (£–££)
- West side bus, Rhodes–Monólithos (Averof St)
- Few
- Monólithos (➤ 20)

Above: *the church in the mountain village of Siána*

STÉGNA

The medium-sized beach at Stégna lies on the coast below the village of Archángelos and is popular with locals as well as visitors. It is reached down a road that winds through a raw landscape of limestone pinnacles and cliffs. High rocky hills frame Stégna to north and south, giving some landscape character to the beach. The beach is a sun trap, but its narrowness means that it can become crowded and development is increasing.

- 43D3
- East coast, 36km south of Rhodes Town
- Seasonal cafés and tavernas (£–££)
- East side bus, Rhodes–Archángelos, daily (Rimini Sq)
- Few

A Drive in the Far South of Rhodes

The far south and west of Rhodes is pleasingly remote, and this drive follows a rewarding route between the mountains and the sea.

Leave Líndos on the Péfkoi road. Bypass Péfkoi (➤ 60), or drop off for a swim, and after about 4km, just before Lárdos (➤ 56), turn left up a short link road, signed Gennádi and Kattavía, then turn left onto the main coast road.

From now on, beach resorts thin out and a more remote rural island begins to emerge. Tempting beaches at Glystra (➤ 49) and Plimíri (➤ 61) are easily reached from the main road.

Pass the pleasant villages of Kiotári (➤ 50) and Gennádi (➤ 48), both with good beaches. Continue to Kattavía (➤ 50), beyond which the road swings to the north and the sea comes into view.

For the next 10km there are virtually no buildings. The shore is lined with grey, pebbly beaches that can be quite breezy.

At Apolakkiá, turn left, signed Monólithos. Continue through pleasant tree-studded countryside to reach Monólithos.

Take some time to explore Monólithos village (➤ 20) for an insight into the rural life of Rhodes away from the tourist attractions.

Turn left at a junction by Cristos Corner Taverna and follow the road to Monólithos castle and then downhill to Fourni if you have time. Return to Monólithos, and from the junction by Cristos Corner retrace your route to Apolakkiá. From the centre of Apolakkiá, take the road, signed Genadi (sic). At a big junction go left, signed Genadi (sic), cross a bridge then continue through low hills to reach a junction with the main coast road at Gennádi. Turn left and return to Líndos via Péfkoi.

Distance
130km

Time
8 hours if beach diversions are made

Start/end point
Líndos
43C2

Lunch
Cristos Corner Taverna (£)
Monólithos
0246 61310

Fourni beach, below Monólithos Castle

43D5
East coast, 4km south of Rhodes Town
Seasonal café and taverna (£–££)
East side bus, Rhodes–Faliráki (Rimini Sq)
Excursion boats from Mandraki Harbour
Few
Faliráki (➤ 48)

Palms on the seafront at Thérmes Kalithéa

THÉRMES KALITHÉA

The rather dilapidated and disused spa complex at Kalithéa still manages to retain an eccentric appeal. Work goes on in a bid to renovate this Italian extravaganza, and in the main complex enough has been done to give a good impression of what the place was like in its heyday. Kalithéa's healing springs were famous as early as the classical period, and the Italians spared no effort in turning the spa into a 1930s Moorish showpiece – a palm-fringed, seaside oasis complete with colonnaded gardens, curving staircases and domed pavilions, the latter in a very poor state at present. A central cupola, supported by pillars, stands over a circular spa pool. There is a small shingle and sand beach and several rocky coves.

43D5
West coast, 8km southwest of Rhodes Town
Numerous tavernas and cafés in village centre and alongside beach (£–££)
West side bus, Rhodes–Paradissi (Averof St)
Few
Ialyssós (➤ 14)
Aug festival

TRIÁNTA

Triánta is a busy and lively village with a reassuring local identity. There is a shingle beach about 0.5km from the main road. It is reached by link roads from the village and is popular in the summer, with windsurfers as well as sun lovers, this being the breezier side of the island. Ancient Triánta was essentially the Bronze Age precursor to classical Ialyssós and throughout the broad agricultural plain that spreads inland behind the village, numerous prehistoric artefacts have been found. Triánta's handsome Church of the Dormition of the Virgin has a splendid baroque bell tower.

TSAMPÍKA

The Tsampíka area has two attractions: a surprisingly undeveloped beach, and the monastery of Panagia Tsampíka, known also as Kyra, a tiny white building perched on top of a huge cone-shaped hill that towers to a height of 287m above the beach. Tsampíka's fine swathe of sand and lack of background buildings are definite pluses, but they ensure the beach's popularity by day and there are watersports available here during the season. The monastery is reached by a concrete road that twists steeply up from the highway, just before the beach access road. You park just beyond the Panoramic Restaurant and finish the journey on foot up winding stone stairs through pine trees. It's a long haul – there are 307 steps, marked at 100-step intervals. The 'monastery' is no more than a tiny chapel and courtyard, but the views are spectacular, and the chapel contains a greatly revered icon of the Annunciation that legend says arrived miraculously and inexplicably from Cyprus.

43D3

East coast, 30km south of Rhodes Town

Seasonal *kantínas* (food and drink stall) and taverna at beach (£). Panoramic Restaurant below monastery (£–££)

East side bus, Rhodes–Archángelos (Rimini Sq)

None at monastery, few at beach

Archángelos (➤ 44), Kolýmpia (➤ 51), Stégna (➤ 66)

Dress soberly when visiting monastery, no photography inside. 8 Sep, Festival during which childless women climb the steps to the monastery to pray for a baby. If they are successful, the child is named Tsambikos or Tsambika

The tiny monastery of Panagia Tsampíka crowns the hill above the beach

VLÍKA

The attractive crescent beach at Vlíka tends to be monopolised by guests from the large hotels that occupy the land behind the shoreline, but there are plenty of facilities here that can be enjoyed by day visitors. To the north of the headland is a 6km shingle beach that runs from the roadside resort of Kalathos to Charáki (➤ 45), fringing Reni Bay.

43C3

East coast, 52km south of Rhodes Town

Seasonal *kantinas* (food and drink stalls) and tavernas behind beach

Few (beach accessible on the level)

Líndos (➤ 57)

DID YOU KNOW?

The first written Law of the Sea was established in Rhodes in classical times. The Romans adopted many tenets of the *Lex Rhodia*, as the Law of the Sea was known, and elements of Rhodian Marine Law still form the basis of modern maritime codes.

The approach to the island by boat reveals Sými's hidden treasure – a 19th-century island town, preserved in almost perfect detail

Sými

The small but mountainous island of Sými lies between the lobster-like claws of Turkish peninsulas. It is a beautiful island, emphatically Greek in nature. The approach by boat to Sými Town reveals a stunning amphitheatre of 19th-century neo-classical houses, pastel-coloured and pedimented – an unexpected and breathtaking sight. Evidence of Sými's remarkable past is seen in the numerous ruined and empty buildings that pepper the older parts of the town. Until the early 20th century the island had a population of over 20,000, and was wealthier even than Rhodes because of its lucrative sponge-diving, shipbuilding and sea trade. Then the island's economy was blighted by a combination of the Italian occupation of the Dodecanese, the war between Greece and Turkey, and a rapid decline in the sponge trade. Emigration on a huge scale followed.

- 42A5 (arrowed from)
- 24km north of Rhodes Island
- Numerous cafés, bars and tavernas in Sými Town (£–£££)
- Hourly bus to Chorió and Pédio from east side of harbour
- Day excursion boats from Rhodes Town, water-taxis to various beaches, May–Oct
- No tourist office, but English-language newspaper *The Sými Visitor* is excellent source of information
- Few
- Sými Festival Jun–Sep. Music, drama, poetry, folk culture. Programme features top Greek performers

Below: *Sými's tradtional skills in boatbuilding are still practised at Haráni*

Today, Sými is flourishing again, as a result of tourism – it is a very popular day trip from Rhodes. The island's steep-sidedness and a lack of water have ensured that over-development has not happened. Apart from during the day when the harbour is very busy, Sými Town and the island's outlying districts emanate a persuasive atmosphere of an older Greece.

SÝMI TOWN ✪✪✪

Sými Town is made up of its lower harbour area, known as Gialós, and the upper, older town known as Chorió. Gialós is, understandably, the busiest part of the town. The

Top: *the view from the top of the Kali Strata*
Above: *one of the many deserted fine houses along the way*

harbour is broad and long, framed by rising land to either side and overlooked by tiers of pastel-coloured houses with neat pediments. Ferries and excursion boats dock at the west quay which is lined with cafés, tavernas, shops, and workshops. The harbourside road leads on from here past hotels and houses to the settlement of Haráni, where small boatyards maintain the tradition of Sými boatbuilding.

The older district of Chorió rises dramatically from the east side of the harbour to where a line of old windmills punctuates the skyline and the ruined castle of the Knights of St John, occupied by the Church of Megali Panagia, crowns the highest point. The best way to approach Chorió is to climb the magnificent stone staircase, the Kali Strata, where the atmospheric shells of abandoned 19th-century mansions line the lower stairs. From higher up the Kali Strata you enter a fascinating world where tempting alleyways lead off to either side into a maze of occupied and unoccupied houses linked by stairways and narrow passages, the whole punctuated with open terraces and squares (► 70, Walk).

42A5 (arrowed from)
14km from Sými Town
Café and taverna (££)
Hire truck from Gialós, 0241 71695
Excursion boats from Rhodes and water-taxis from Gialós

MONÍ TAXÍARCHAS MICHAEL PANORMÍTIS ✪✪

The monastery of Panormítis lies at the far southern tip of Sými and is an extremely popular destination for excursion boats. It can be reached by rough road from Sými Town, but this involves a hard six-hour walk or travel by hired truck. The most convenient – and dramatic – approach is from the sea into the horseshoe-shaped bay that lies in front of Panormítis below pine-covered hills. The 18th-

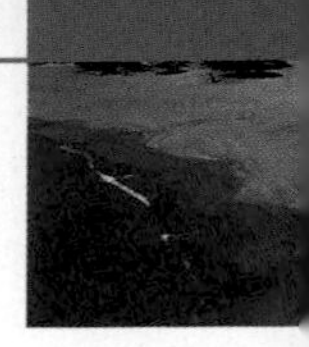

century monastery is a huge building, almost Venetian in style. Its tall, baroque bell tower dominates the long white facade of the main building. The inner courtyard contains the free-standing church, which has a superb carved wooden altar screen and numerous gold and silver lamps, as well as a silver-leafed representation of the Archangel Michael, patron saint of Sými and protector of sailors. There is a small museum, with an exhibition of various curiosities and artefacts.

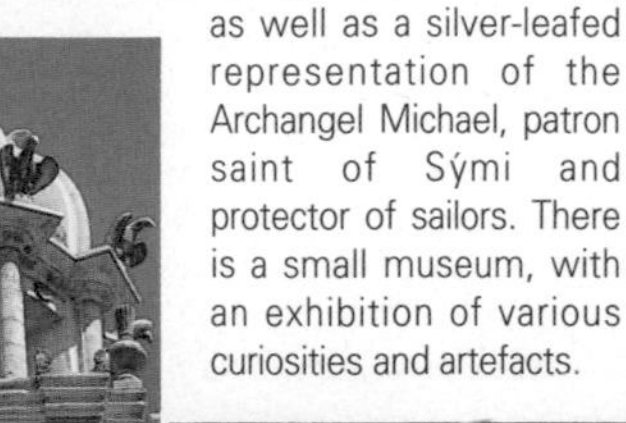

The impressive sweep of the monastery building with (inset) a detail from the cupola

PÉDIO

The small village of Pédio lies on the south side of the high promontory that flanks Sými Town. It still retains its engaging character as a fishing village from where small boats work the inshore waters. There is a narrow shingly beach on the waterfront, but it takes half an hour to walk along the path across the rocky hillside from the south end of the village to the pleasant sandy beach of Ágios Nikólaos. A 20-minute walk along a path from the north end of the village leads to the shingle beach of Ágios Marína. Both beaches become very busy in summer, as crowded water-taxis arrive from Sými Town.

- 42A5 (arrowed from)
- 3km from Sými Town
- Café-bars and tavernas
- Hourly bus from Gialós
- Water-taxis from Gialós
- None

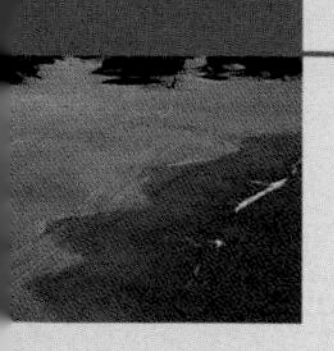

The Stone Steps of Chorió

Distance
2.5km

Time
3 hours allowing for visits to museum and churches

Start point
Scala Square, Gialós

End point
Gialós

Lunch
Cafés on approach to museum (£)

This walk links the two great stone staircases of Chorió and visits Sými's museum and several churches.

From Scala Square climb the broad steps of the Kali Strata. Follow prominent signs (blue arrows) to the museum, through a series of alleyways.

The museum contains an excellent collection of Byzantine and medieval artefacts. Near by is the restored 18th-century Chatziagapitos Mansion.

Walk straight ahead from the museum doorway past a telegraph pole. Go beneath an arch, then climb steps by a sign for 'Castle'. Pass a house with blue-painted steps, then follow a narrow alley. At a junction keep right, go down two steps to an open square in front of the handsome Church of Ágios Athanosios.

A small chapel just below the Church of Megali Panagia

Like all of Sými's churches, St Athanosios is brightly painted and immaculate.

*Go down curved steps on the far side of the square, then turn left at a junction. Keep straight ahead at the telegraph pole, then at a T-junction go left. At the next junction go right to reach another immaculate church. Go up the steps to the left of the church, then turn right, then left. Keep ahead to where a sharp turn right leads up some steps. Go up left to reach the castle (*Kastro*).*

The site of the old castle is dominated by the Church of Megali Panagia, a replacement of a previous church destroyed during World War II. One of the church bells is the nose-cone of a bomb.

Retrace your steps from the church, then go down left to reach another church with a tall bell tower. Turn right down more steps, then go left. Follow a road round the hillside to reach another church, from where steps lead down to the top of the Katarraktis, Chorió's second great stone stairway that leads down to Gialós.

Where To...

Above: *pottery from Líndos*
Right: *traditional costume – and a traditional Rhodian welcome*

Rhodes Town

Prices
Approximate prices for a full meal with a glass of wine.
£ = under €12
££ = €12–€22
£££ = over €22

Choosing a Restaurant
In main tourist areas, you will be 'touted' unrelentingly as you stroll by restaurants and a running commentary is *de rigeur* from taverna front men if you dare stop to study the display menu. This can be annoying, but patience and courtesy is your best response. Look for the busiest tavernas, especially those patronised by locals and where they do not have cushioned seats, waiters in uniform dress or other lavish trimmings.

Angeli Di Roma (££)
A stylish restaurant with an exciting menu and excellent wine list. Try delicious mushrooms with crab filling for starters, followed by Angeli di Roma steak with shrimp sauce, then spoil yourself with strawberry-filled meringue nest.
62 Sof Venizelou St, New Town 0241 30044 Lunch, dinner

Cairo Café (£)
Good central café at heart of New Town shopping district. Plentiful breakfast buffet. Also tasty snacks and great selection of 14 different coffee brands.
12 Eth Makariou St, New Town 0241 75362 8PM– 1AM

Cavalliere (£)
Classy *gelateria* (ice cream parlour) and patisserie. Standard pizzas and other snacks available, but also has a selection of wickedly tasty pastries and cakes, and a good wine and liquor list.
Ioannou Kazouli St, New Town 0241 22932 All day

Cleo's (££–££)
Fine *nouvelle cuisine*, essentially Italian but with other influences, in this sophisticated restaurant. Good menu includes *tagliatelle al salmone* and tasty *carpaccio* with some delicious sweets. Reservations advised.
17 Ágios Fanoúriou St, Old Town 0241 28415 7–midnight, Apr–Oct

El Divino (£)
Music café favoured by smart young Rhodians. Good location in old Italian mansion, set back from the street with a large outside terrace.
5 Alex Diakou St (corner of Papagou) 0241 39040/41 All day

Fashion House Café (£)
Busy, popular café-bar in New Town's liveliest street. Serves good snacks and has a huge range of hot and cold drinks from coffee to beers, wines and spirits.
46b Amerikis St, New Town 0241 78369 Lunch, dinner

Hatzikelis (££–£££)
Stylish Greek decor in restaurant favoured by equally stylish locals. Excellent fish dishes, good *mezédhes* (starters) and meat dishes.
9 Solomou Alhadef St, Old Town 0241 27215 Lunch, dinner

Hippocrates (££)
Old Town restaurant with fine *hokhláki* (pebble mosaic) floor. Good fish and extensive *mezédhes*. Excellent wine list – try top end red and white Lazariois, or the reasonable house wine and retsina.
Evripidou St, Old Town 11AM–midnight

India Restaurant (£-££)
Excellent Indian cuisine at this New Town restaurant where there is a huge selection of main courses to choose from. Meat, fish and vegetarian dishes on offer and fine sauces.
16 Konstantopedos St (off Ionos Dragoumi St), New Town 0241 38395 6:30–late. Closed Mon

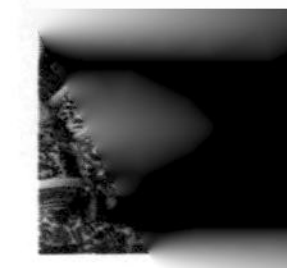

Internet Café (£)
At the heart of New Town; a music and internet café with PCs and email facilities.
✉ 7 Dimokratias St, New Town ☎ 0241 27502; email: admin@rockstyle.gr Web site: www.rockstyle.gr 🕑 All day

Kon Tiki (££)
Floating restaurant, moored in Mandraki Harbour. Good selection of fish dishes and caters for meat eaters and vegetarians. Italian cuisine also. Lavish breakfasts available from 9AM.
✉ Mandraki Harbour, New Town ☎ 0241 22477 🕑 9AM–late

Marco Polo Café (££)
Wonderful location in very old building that measures the history of Rhodes Old Town from Byzantine times, through the era of the Knights to the Turkish period. Enjoy light meals and drinks in fine surroundings.
✉ 40–42 Ágios Fanoúriou St, Old Town ☎ 0241 37889 🕑 All day

Mike's (£)
Good little fish restaurant, tucked away in an alley running parallel to Sokratous St and reached along a lane directly opposite Taverne Alexis (➤ below). Great alternative if you're low on funds and fashion.
✉ Off Sokratous St, Old Town 🕑 Lunch, dinner

Mollye's Diner (£)
Varied menu to please all tastes from pasta eaters to vegetarians. Also serves classic English breakfasts and for lunch or dinner battered haddock, bangers and mash, and steak pie.
✉ 25 Ionos Dragoumi St, New Town ☎ 0241 75328 🕑 9:00AM–11PM daily

Nisiros (££)
Standard fare in this big taverna-restaurant at the heart of the finest medieval street in the Old Town. Prices tend to be slightly atmospheric, to match the setting.
✉ 45–7 Ágios Fanoúriou St, Old Town ☎ 0241 31471 🕑 Lunch, dinner

Romeo Taverna & Grill (££)
Big menu of Greek and Eastern Mediterranean dishes at this long-established restaurant, located in old builidng off Sokratous St. Good selection of *mezédhes* (starters) and casseroled or foil-wrapped, grilled main dishes. Wine list features Rhodian Villaré as well as reasonable house wine. Live Greek music.
✉ 7–9 Menekleous St, Old Town ☎ 0241 25186 🕑 All day. Last orders 1AM

Taverne Alexis (££–£££)
A superb *psarotaverna* (fish restaurant) at the heart of busy Sokratous St. Frequented by fashionable Greeks, and pricy. You can order what you want to be prepared from a cold slab display inside. Wine list is in keeping with quality – and price. Garden restaurant area to supplement the streetside seating. Reservations essential.
✉ 18 Sokratous St (on corner with Aristomenous St), Old Town ☎ 0241 29347; fax 0241 29347 🕑 Lunch, dinner. Closed Sun except in Aug

Yiannis Taverna (£)
Popular, family-run taverna without frills, but with excellent food and drink and outstanding value. The friendly host Yiannis Balaskas and his staff never seem to stop, as they serve up classic Greek dishes with great courtesy.
✉ 41 Platonas St, off Sokratous St, Old Town ☎ 0241 36535 🕑 10AM–midnight

Fast Food
In Rhodes fast food has become blandly international, but Greek snacks can be much more satisfying. Try *tiropita* (cheese pie) or *spanakopita* (spinach pie with cheese), delicious – and addictive – when fresh. *Gyros* are wonderfully tasty Greek kebabs sold from open-fronted shop stalls where sizzling layers of meat on a vertical spit revolve in front of a grill. Pieces of meat are sliced directly from the *gyro* onto pitta bread, and garnish, onions, tomatoes and chips are added.

Tips
There is usually a service charge built into the bill in town restaurants and tavernas, and waiters do not overtly expect tips. If you wish to tip for especially good service and courtesy then 10 per cent is adequate.

Booking
It is advisable to book a table in popular town restaurants and in those with high reputations. In rural areas, booking by phone is often irrelevant, however. Country tavernas will always find a place, even if it is in their own garden, or an overspill into the village square.

Rhodes and Sými

Coffee
Coffee-drinking makes for essential punctuation marks in the Greek day. For the conservative taste Nescafé (or 'Nes') is recognised universally to mean instant coffee. But you should try *kafés Ellinika*, Greek coffee, for the authentic taste of the country. It is made from thick grounds and is served in small cups and may be *sketo* (unsweetened), *metrio* (medium sweet) or *glyko* (sweetened). Sip slowly and alternate with accompanying cool water, or better still, a glass of *oúzo*. An ideal thirst quencher is *kafés frappé*, a long glass of iced coffee. Most places will bring a glass of water with *kafés frappé*, and you can prolong the drink by topping up with the water.

Take Note
In most restaurants and tavernas you will be given a bill that at least indicates the overall price of your meal, though it may not be itemised. Keep a check against the menu price if you feel concerned about possible overcharging. The people of Rhodes, like most Greeks, are instinctively honest and fair minded, but mistakes can happen.

Around the Island

Archángelos

Savas (££)
A friendly and authentic atmosphere in this pleasant taverna right on the main street. Menu includes top of the range lobster, octopus in wine, stuffed squid and reliable meat dishes. Quite pricey, but excellent. Rhodian wines available as well as decent and inexpensive house wine.
Archángelos 0244 23125 Lunch, dinner

Charáki

Chef Tommy's (££)
Well-run taverna with excellent fish dishes, although top end delicacies are frozen imports. Try grilled swordfish. Good *mezédhes* include pumpkin and courgette balls. Decent wine list.
Charáki (alongside car park) Lunch, dinner

Falaráki

La Strada (£–££)
Popular Italian restaurant with huge selection. Pizza, pasta and marvellous variety of fish and meat dishes. Tasty desserts include Italian ice-cream and *crème caramel*.
Líndos Ave 0241 85878 All day

Gennádi

Mama's Kitchen (££)
Very pleasant restaurant at heart of village. Great selection of Greek dishes. Try *pitaroudia*, fried chick peas, or *soutzoukakia* meatballs in delicious sauce. Pizza fanciers are well-catered for too. Good selection of Rhodian wines.
Gennádi 0244 43547 Lunch, dinner

Ialyssós

Stani Pool Cafe (£)
Very pleasant, if bland, café-bar with outside swimming pool overlooking reasonable beach. General snacks, but ice-cream, pastries and sweetmeats are the real attraction. Indulge in apple pie, yoghurt and honey, and *baklavás* (pastry with honey and nuts).
Shopping Centre, Rodoslan, Iraklidon St, Ialyssós 0241 96422

Net Club (£)
An Internet café with all facilities provided including net-surfing, PC games and email.
8 N Plastira St, Ialyssós 0241 98100; email: admin@net-club.gr All day

Kameíros

Taverna Old Kameíros (£)
Standard Greek cooking is on the menu at this roadside taverna, but choose one of the tasty fish dishes done in oil or grilled for a good value meal. There's also a wide selection of salads.
Kameíros 0241 40012 Lunch, dinner

Kameíros Skala

Althaimeni (££)
This fish restaurant comes well recommended, being very popular with the locals. A sunny outdoor terrace overlooks the fishing harbour. A big menu includes such expensive treats as red mullet and lobster. For starters try fried aubergines. Also good salads and dips.
Kameíros 0246 31303 Lunch, dinner

Kiotári

La Strada (£)
Straightforward beachside taverna with good fish dishes and general Greek cuisine. Located oppposite the Rock of One Thousand Stakes (▶ 50).
Kiotári beach ☎ 0244 47187 ⏲ 10AM–midnight

Kolýmpia

To Limanaki (£)
Long-established fish taverna, in a good position overlooking beach. There's even an old fishing boat beached alongside to add to the atmosphere.
Kolýmpia ☎ 0241 56240 ⏲ All day

Líndos

Agostinos (££)
Worthwhile taverna on the southern edge of the village just below the Stavri Square car park. Stunning view of Acropolis from terrace – barring occasional TV aerials.
Líndos ⏲ Lunch, dinner

Restaurant Líndos (££)
Charming, well-run restaurant at the heart of Líndos. It seems to climb ever higher through successive roof levels with superb views of the Acropolis. Try and book a table at the highest 'crow's nest' level, from where you can keep a look out for pirates while you enjoy the good Greek cuisine and fine wines.
Líndos ☎ 0244 31640 ⏲ 10:30AM–11PM

Monólithos

Cristos Corner (£)
Unmissable on the approach road into Monólithos. Run by the genial Cristos Fanarakis, this classic rural taverna offers good *mezédhes* and charcoal grilled main dishes. Try yoghurt with the delicious local honey for dessert.
Monólithos ☎ 0246 61310 ⏲ Lunch, dinner

Péfkoi

Shanghai Chinese Restaurant (££)
If you want a change from Greek cuisine try this Chinese. Also take-away service.
Péfkoi, south junction ☎ 0244 48217 ⏲ Lunch, dinner

Sými

Fish Restaurant Manos (££)
Excellent fish restaurant offering big menu that includes oysters, clams, king prawns, lobster, and much more. Fish soup of the day is a good choice. Reservations advised.
Harbourside, Gialós ☎ 0241 72429 ⏲ Lunch, dinner

Georgio's (£)
High up the Kali Strata, Georgio's is a taverna with character – and characters in plenty. Georgio himself brings a wealth of 'life experience' to the job and the food's quite good too. The fish soup makes an excellent starter, but then you may get it as a finisher.
Kali Strata, Chorió ☎ 0241 71984 ⏲ Most days

Hellenikon (££)
An impressive list of over 140 Greek vintages from its unique cellar enhances this restaurant's fine menu of fish and meat dishes, pastas, grills and vegetarian choice.
Town Square ☎ 0241 72455 ⏲ Dinner

Taverna Amoni (£)
Rewarding taverna with quality traditional Greek cuisine and good wine list. Enjoy stuffed vine leaves as just one of the classic dishes on offer.
Town Square, Gialós ☎ 0241 72540 ⏲ Lunch, dinner

Vegetarian and Vegan Options

Greeks are great meat and fish eaters although they have a marvellous tradition of vegetable cooking too. If you eat fish rather than meat, then you will be spoiled for choice, but if you are a strict vegetable eater you should concentrate on salads and on a variety of *mezédhes* (starters) from which you can make more than a filling meal. Try *manitaria* (mushrooms), *dolmadakia* (vine leaves stuffed with rice), *saganaki* (cheese fried in oil) and *spanokeftedes* (spinach balls with cheese). Be wary of mixed dishes such as pasta with vegetables or vegetable casserole. Small pieces of meat are often mixed in with such dishes. Dedicated vegetarian menus are increasingly on offer in main centres such as Rhodes Town.

Drink

For non wine and beer drinkers, there's no greater standby than cool water, and bottled water is universally available. Or you can enjoy orange juice – in the best cafés and restaurants this should be made from fresh oranges and is delicious. Soft drinks are available in international brands, but be careful with some Greek soft drinks. Although youngsters won't care, drinks such as *portokalada* (fizzy orange) and lemon-flavoured *lemonada* are very sweet.

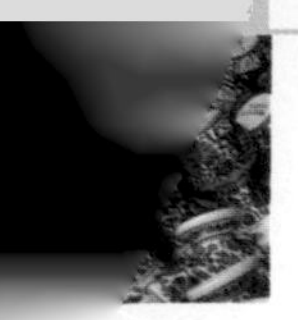

Rhodes Town

Prices
Approximate price for a double room for one night. (Prices are for the room not per person.)
£ = under €35
££ = €35–€60
£££ = over €60

Passports and Payment
Reception will ask for a passport when you register at a hotel or pension. This is simply to record details and your passport should be returned as soon as this is done. Payment by credit card is accepted at most upper grade hotels in towns and larger resorts. Rural *pensions* and small hotels usually prefer to deal in cash. There are easily located cash machines in Rhodes New Town and at the foot of Ippotón in the Old Town.

Safety and Security
Lifts in Greek hotels often do not have cabin doors. The shaft on the doorway side is thus unprotected when the lift is moving, so take extreme care, especially of young children. Most reputable hotels are secure and most have a safe where you can place small items of value.

Best Western Plaza Hotel (£££)
Top-of-range hotel with comfortable rooms and luxury fittings. Quite good soundproofing. Breakfast buffet is outstanding.
✉ 7 Ierou Lochou St, New Town ☎ 0241 22501; fax 0241 22544; e-mail: plaza@otenet.gr Website: www.rhodes-plaza.com

Hermes Hotel (££)
A well-situated, fairly plain and simple, mid-range hotel with some rooms looking over Mandraki Harbour. Rooms are en suite and have air-conditioning, telephone and TV. Simple breakfast included in price.
✉ 5 Plastira St, New Town ☎ 0241 27677; fax 0241 33160

Hotel Anastasia (££)
A pleasant, family-run hotel with character. Located in leafy garden area off main street. Straightforward high-ceilinged rooms. Outside breakfast area beneath hibiscus canopy. Bar.
✉ 46 28 Oktovriou St, New Town ☎ 0241 28007; fax 0241 21815

Hotel Andreas (££)
Located at the heart of the Old Town, this delightful, and very popular, small hotel has great views across the rooftops from its terraces and bar.
✉ 28d Omirou St, Old Town ☎ 0241 34156; fax 0241 74285 ⌚ Mid-Mar to Oct

Hotel Despo (££)
A very well run hotel at the heart of the commercial district. Medium-sized establishment; rooms with central heating.
✉ 40 Gr Lampraki St, New Town ☎ 0241 22571

Manousos (££)
Modern hotel with facilities matching those of more expensive establishments, including swimming pool, gym and sauna. Excellent breakfasts.
✉ 25 G Leontos St, New Town ☎ 0241 22741; fax 0241 28834

New Village Inn (££)
This pleasant oasis at the heart of the New Town hotel area is tucked away down a narrow alleyway, and entered through an attractive courtyard. There is a separate charge for breakfast. Licensed.
✉ 10 Konstantopedos St, New Town ☎ 0241 34937; email: newvillageinn@rho.forthnet.gr

St Nikolas (££)
Handsome Old Town building in hidden corner. Wonderful ambience includes inner courtyard with resident tortoise. A selection of very different types of room is available, most with character. Excellent facilities. Good breakfast with view, on roof garden.
✉ 61 Ippodamou St, Old Town ☎ 0241 34561; fax 0241 32034

Spartalis (££)
A large modern hotel at the centre of the commercial district, overlooking Mandraki Harbour. Pleasant and well maintained, with en suite rooms. Bar.
✉ 2 Plastira St, New Town ☎ 0241 24371/27670; fax 0241 20406 ⌚ May–Oct

Rhodes and Sými

Around the Island

Afántou

Oasis (£–££)

Bungalow and studio-type accommodation are available at this medium-size hotel. Well-suited to families, and quite handy for beaches. Facilities include a swimming pool, with a separate pool for children.

Afántou 0241 51771-5; fax 0241 51770; email: oasis-bungalows@rho.forthnet.gr Apr–Oct

Archángelos

Calimera Porto Angeli (£££)

A luxury hotel, part of the Calimera Aktivhotels chain. Offering good facilities, the hotel has its own sizeable pool, which is just as well, because the beach near by is not the most salubrious.

Stegna beach, Archángelos 0244 24000-4; fax 0244 22121 Apr–Oct

Asklipeío

Agapitos (£)

A few rooms available above the Agapitos Restaurant. Very friendly owners.

Asklipeío 0244 47255 Apr–Oct

Charáki

Anthony's (££)

Pleasant apartment rooms located at north end of beachside promenade, with the attractive setting of the castle behind.

Charáki 0244 51861 Apr–Oct

Faliráki

Esperides Beach Hotel (££)

A large, modern beach-front hotel with its own swimming pool. Well equipped for family holidays and offering every facility, including a cocktail bar, disco, mini-market, coffee bar, poolside taverna, tennis courts, mini-golf and volleyball. For youngsters there are numerous attractions ranging from bumper cars to a Venturer simulator.

Faliráki 0241 85267; fax 0241 85079 Apr–Oct

Gennádi

Effie's Dreams (£)

Tucked away in quiet tree shaded area at the back of the village, just below the Church of Ágios Ioannis. Run by local family, there is a café/snackbar attached and internet facilities.

Gennádi 0244 43205; fax 0244 43437; email dreams@srh.forthnet.gr

Ixiá

Ródos Palace (£££)

Huge, luxury hotel noted for its conference facilities and for hosting international meetings. All facilities that you would expect and a choice of rooms, suites and bungalows.

Trianton Ave, Ixiá 0241 25222; fax 0241 21511; email info@rodos-palace.gr; Website: www.rodos-palace.gr Apr–Oct

Kolýmpia

Hotel Relax (£)

Small, pleasant hotel with palm trees and gardens in front. Own swimming pool, but a touch public as it's alongside approach road to beach. Air-conditioning. Block-booked by mainly German charters but worth trying by independents.

Kolýmpia 0241 56220; fax 0241 56245 Apr–Oct

Classification

Hotel rooms are graded by Greek Tourist police into categories, starting at L for Luxury, then grading from A to E in descending order of facilities and quality, but not necessarily of character. By law, all hotel rooms must display low, mid and high season rates on a card which is fixed to the inside of the room door. During the low season especially, you can often negotiate extremely favourable discounts; more so if you stay for several nights.

Availability

Rhodes has a large number of hotel rooms and studio and apartments for rent, but many are seasonal and are block-booked by charter companies. In peak season, Rhodes New Town is usually the best place to find a room. Hotels and pensions in the Old Town are, by nature, small establishments and rooms can be difficult to find here in the high season. In rural areas, rooms are often taken up in the high season, but villagers will often find somewhere for you to stay if you are stranded. During the low season, between November and Easter, resort and village hotels and apartments are often closed, but early in the year you will often find excellent places to stay, especially where the owners live adjacent to the premises. Ask at local shops – founts of all knowledge.

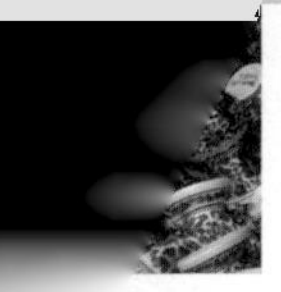

Breakfast
Breakfast is usually included in the room price at more expensive hotels; it can be a lavish buffet of fruit juices, yoghurt, peaches, cereal, cold meats, cheeses and eggs. In less expensive establishments, breakfast might be simply 'continental', with rather dry croissants, rolls and cake. But you will always find a breakfast to suit you in a café or restaurant.

Getting About
Bus services on Rhodes are generally reliable, but a hire car is the best way of exploring the rural areas. There are numerous rental options ranging from international names to local outfits, many of which offer excellent deals. Always check round the vehicle for existing dents or scratches. Be aware that some Rhodian roads, indicated on maps as being surfaced, can turn out to be thudding nightmares of potholes and vestigial tarmac. Drive extremely slowly at night: deep holes, and even road works, are not always clearly signed. Be wary in a stand-off at constricted sections of road, especially if an on-coming vehicle waves you on – the local driver behind you may already be pulling out impatiently, and probably into your side, as you pull out. Flashing headlights mean that the approaching driver is coming ahead, not that he is inviting you to do so.

Lachaniá

Hotel Lachaniá (£)
Small, pleasant hotel in very quiet location on approach road to village. Nearest beach some distance away so own transport advisable.
✉ Lachaniá ☎ 0244 46129
🕐 Apr–Oct

Ladikó

Hotel Cathrin (££-£££)

Very smart and beautifully located hotel, entirely on its own. Caters well for families and has a swimming pool, children's pool and playroom.
✉ Ladikó ☎ 0241 85881; fax 0241 85624 🕐 Apr–Oct

Líndos

Domna Studios (££)
Pleasant complex of self-catering rooms with superb view of Acropolis. Right at the top of the village, but worth the short climb.
✉ Líndos village ☎ 0244 31714; fax 0244 31714

Líndos Royal Village (££–£££)
Custom-built hotel some distance from Líndos itself. Dominates Vryhi Beach, but completely self-contained and with a tiny bay below. Superb facilities and all activities catered for.
✉ Líndos ☎ 0244 32000; fax 0244 32007 🕐 Apr–Oct

Monólithos

Cristos Corner (£)
A couple of rooms are available at this popular restaurant-bar where you won't be short of good company and plenty of food.
✉ Monólithos ☎ 0246 61310

Péfkoi

Thalia Hotel (££)
Pleasant, family hotel near beach, with own pool, restaurant and mini-market.
✉ Péfkoi ☎ 0244 48108
🕐 Apr–Oct

Prasonísi

Oasis (£)
Rooms are available at the Oasis Restaurant and Café Bar at the entrance to the vast, flat sandy beach of Prasonísi. If you like wide open spaces for breakfast, this is the place.
✉ Prasonísi ☎ 0244 91031
🕐 Apr–Oct

Sými

Hotel Aliki (££–£££)
Located north of the quayside clock tower on road to Haráni. A historic building with views to seaward from front rooms.
✉ Gialós ☎ 0241 71655; fax 0241 71665

Hotel Fiona (££)
Pleasant small hotel with good facilities. Unrivalled position with great sea views from front-facing rooms.
✉ Top of Kali Strata, Chorió ☎ & fax 0241 72088; email symi-vis@otenet.gr; Website: www.symivisitor.com

Titika (££)
Small complex of pleasant en suite rooms with attached kitchen in refurbished house, tucked away beyond the head of the harbour. Very steep steps on approach.
✉ Gialós (enquire at Kostas Maliakas's shop, opposite kiosk on south side of harbour bridge) ☎ 0241 71501; fax 0241 72301

Vlíka

Atrium Palace (£££)
Luxury hotel in spectacular kitsch design. Utterly exclusive, since no other buildings within sight. Pool complex complete with exotic palms, waterfalls, and bridges. Huge adjoining beach.
✉ Kalathos Beach ☎ 0244 31601/31622; fax 0244 31600; email: atrium@otenet.gr
🕐 Apr–Oct

Shopping Directory

Arts and Crafts

Rhodes Town

Aladdin's Gallery
Beautiful handmade carpets and rugs. Specialises in *flocati*, luxurious carpets made from sheep's wool; they can be used also as a kind of duvet.
✉ 70 Ág Fanoúriou St, Old Town ☎ & fax 0241 24011

Kalogirou Art
A superb collection of Rhodian antiques and artefacts including carpets and lace work, furnishings, paintings, all housed in a handsome old building only a few steps away from the Palace of the Grand Masters.
✉ 30 Panetiou St, Old Town ☎ 0241 35900; fax 0241 73131

Kyriakos K Hartofilis
Hand-painted Byzantine icons for sale in this workshop outlet. The artist can be seen at work in the shop.
✉ 81 Sokratous St, Old Town ☎ 0241 22153

Marco Polo Gallery
Stylish art gallery selling Rhodian paintings and prints.
✉ 76 Ág Fanoúriou St, Old Town ☎ & fax 0241 29115

Nikos B Minas
Good selection of pottery of various styles.
✉ 142 Sokratous St, Old Town ☎ 0241 22047

Pazari
Handmade carpets produced at the heart of the Old Jewish Quarter. Working loom often seen in action.
✉ 1 Aristotelous and Dimokritou St, Old Town ☎ 0241 36522

Émponas

Chrysanthe Orfanou
A standard shop front leads to a wonderful collection of rugs, hats and other bits and pieces. Friendly Chrysanthe stitches fabrics in the sunlight and works at her carpet-weaving loom.
✉ Church Square

Siána

Acramitis
Everything that Siána produces is available in this craft shop. A good selection of ceramics, footwear, clothing and attractive sisal-weave bags in great colours and designs. Delicious local honey and the local grape distillate *soumá* also on sale.
✉ Main St ☎ 0246 61385

Shops for Children

Rhodes Town

Scarpino
Children's shoe shop with lots of different styles.
✉ 13 Plastira St, New Town ☎ 0241 37280

The Cartoon Store
Hold back the youngsters in this bright and colourful shop that specialises in classic and modern cartoon themes. Clothes, posters, toys, games, dolls, all featuring cartoon motifs.
✉ 4 Alexandrou Diakou St, New Town ☎ & fax 0241 70210

Fashion Stores

Rhodes Town

Ageliniou
Good selection of leather goods, including handbags, belts, wallets and sandals.
✉ 13 Ionos Dragoumi St, New Town ☎ 0241 39560

Security
The high level of honesty among Greeks in general means that you rarely feel threatened. Take great care of your cash, credit cards and passports however, especially when shopping. It is useful, and reassuring, to have a secure inside pocket, inside shoulder pouch, or inside waist pouch next to the skin, in which your essentials are always carried.

Parking
Do not try to emulate the astonishing parking skills of local drivers, who are expert at casual parking. In Rhodes Town the most convenient parking areas are on Eleftherias Street, alongside Mandraki Harbour. There is a pay zoning system that your rental agent should explain to you. In some villages there are convenient car parks. In larger villages it pays to park on the outskirts, especially during the busy morning and early evening periods.

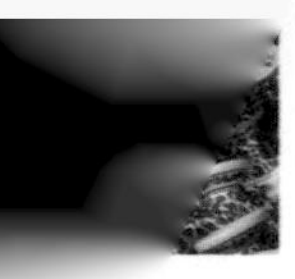

Newspapers and Magazines

Rhodes New Town is the best source for foreign newspapers and magazines. There are several shops throughout the commercial and hotel centre that stock newspapers, but a good source can be found at the kiosks that stand at either side of the main entrance to the New Market on Eleftherias Street, facing Mandraki Harbour. A useful source of information is the advertising publication *Ródos News*, available in English and German editions from tourist information centres.

di piu
Trendy salon, featuring Dolce & Gabbana, Gaultier, Moschino and Krizia jeans and much more.
✉ 46 Alexandrou Diakou St, New Town ☎ 0241 38879

Harley Davidson
Mainly HD brand clothes. Good selection of leather jackets, bags etc. Centrepiece gleaming HD bike puts you in the mood for smart *après* biking gear.
✉ 10 Alexandrou Diakou St, New Town ☎ 0241 78078

Fred Perry
Sportswear from various Greek and European fashion houses such as Lacoste. Quite pricey, but occasional bargains can be found.
✉ 12 Plastira St, New Town ☎ 0241 22217

Roubeti Uomo
Chic fashion shop stocking top named brands such as Versace, Joop, Armani and Gianfranco Ferre.
✉ 6 Kiprou Square, New Town ☎ 0241 75712; fax 0241 32545

Stephanie Boutique
Small clothes shop specialising in ethnic-inspired designs and colours.
✉ 11 Sokratous St, Old Town ☎ 0241 33188

Tommy Hilfiger
International chic to make you feel at home – if international chic is your home...
✉ 46 Grigorious Lanbraki, New Town ☎ 0241 24482

Food & Drink

Rhodes Town

The Green Shop
Amidst the unrelenting ranks of Sokratous gift shops this little shop sells olive oil, herbs, spices, honey and Greek specialities.
✉ 162–4 Sokratous St, Old Town ☎ 0241 77934

Mike's Zaharaplasto
Mouthwatering, hugely indulgent treat for the sweet of tooth. Try *melekouni*, a sesame seed biscuit with honey, or *moshopougi*, a pastry filled with almonds and spice and covered with icing sugar. Also big selection of ice-creams.
✉ Sof Venizelou St, New Town ☎ 0241 66510

Papadopoulos Liqueur Store
Going strong for over 60 years, this New Market shop has a dazzling selection of spirits and liqueurs.
✉ 42 Averof St, New Market New Town ☎ 0241 27485

Pappou Department Store and Supermarket
Very useful basement supermarket in this big store that also has large selection of hardware, stationery, perfumery, and drink on main floor. Supermarket has everything you might need in terms of food.
✉ 7 25 Martiou St, New Town ☎ 0241 24286

Voyatzis & Co
Wonderful old-fashioned shop selling real coffee, nuts, wine and liquor. Endearing atmosphere. Also sells pastries – try the incredibly addictive *mousta*, made from grapes with a walnut centre. You'll be hooked for life.
✉ 30 Averof St, New Market, New Town ☎ 0241 25908

Around the Island

Lárdos

Lárdos Fish Market
If you're self-catering, head for this well-stocked market with its excellent selection of fresh fish and sea food.
✉ Lárdos ☎ 0244 44013
🕑 Mon–Sat 7–2, 5–9

Líndos

Gelo Blu

Mouthwatering Italian ice-cream at the heart of Líndos. Everything from pistachio flavour to standard vanilla, as it really should taste.

Líndos 0244 31671

Petaloúdes

Anastasia Triantafillou Vineyard and Wine Cellar

This independent (and very friendly) winery has superb vintages from organically produced local Athiri grapes and Cabernet Sauvignon. Every bottle is good, but splash out on Kalos Aygos, the vineyard's finest. They also produce superb moscatel.

Petaloúdes (on approach road from main west coast road. Signed on right-hand side of road along track) 0241 82041 Daily 10–8

Gifts

Rhodes Town

Artistik

Old Town shop selling a good selection of ceramics, jewellery, and art objects that have a bit more style than many souvenir shops, but with prices to match.

9 Ippodamou St, Old Town 0241 25954

Robylen

Lots of brightly painted wooden gift items, jewellery and ethnic-style clothing.

8 Plastira St, New Town 0241 78289

Around the Island

Lárdos

Athina Tourist Shop

On the main approach to the town from the coast road, on the outskirts of Lárdos. Everything from beach gear, toys, souvenirs, kitsch statues, ceramics and leatherware.

Lárdos 0244 44005 Mon–Sat 9:30am–10pm, Sun 10:30–2, 5–10

Líndos

Olympic Tourist Shop

The best stocked of the many tourist shops that line the approaches to the Acropolis. This one is in the lane branching left on your way down and stocks a wide range of ceramics, jewellery and souvenirs.

Líndos 0244 31355

Sými

Afrothiti

Worthwhile and often unusual gifts.

Gialós (in street behind harbour front near Church of St John)

Pegasus Gift Shop

Another good gift shop in the harbour area.

Gialós (same street as Afrothiti)

Jewellery

Rhodes Town

E Karidis Jewellery

Good selection of gold and silver watches and jewellery.

61 Ermou St, Old Town & fax 0241 20381

Ródos Silver

Wide selection of silver jewellery and gifts.

22 Protogenous St, Old Town 0241 24950

Photography

Rhodes Town

Sakellaridis Photo Shop

Best selection of gear and films in Rhodes; processing also available.

5a Ionos Dragoumi St, New Town 0241 25575 4-6 Ethnarhou Makariou St, New Town 0241 27361

Public Toilets

Rhodes Town is well-supplied with public toile[ts] that have quite a high standard of cleanliness. Restaurants and tavernas must have toilets by law. Male and female 'figure signs' are usually in place. The Greek for Gents is *andron* and for Ladies it is *gynaikon*. Be prepared; toilets, public or otherwise, do not always have toilet paper available. In Rhodes the circumference of waste pipes is small and outlets are easily blocked by toilet paper and other items. Please comply with local custom, however fastidious you may feel, and dispose of used toilet paper in receptacles that are supplied in all toilets.

Music, Nightlife & Theatre

…d Manners and …gal Matters
…is neither courteous nor sensible to make disparaging remarks about Greek religion, culture or the Greek state. Such behaviour may be judged as constituting an offence and may be treated as such by the police.
Use of recreational drugs and supplying drugs of any kind is considered to be a major crime in Greece. Being found guilty of supplying even small amounts of drugs for personal use may result in a very long prison sentence.

Photography
Holiday photographs are essential memories to take home from Rhodes. You can photograph virtually anything that takes your fancy without annoying people, but near military installations notices will warn against taking photographs. Heed such warnings very carefully and make sure that such installations are not accidentally included in the background to an innocent photograph. In churches, monasteries and museums there is often a strict ruling against photography.

Rhodes Town

Casino Rhodos
A major entertainment venue with 300 slot machines and a gaming room with 30 tables offering American roulette, blackjack and Caribbean stud poker. Top class entertainment and cuisine in the Crystal Club. Fairly relaxed dress code, but no jeans or shorts.
✉ Hotel Grande Albergo delle Rosa, 4 Georgiou Papanikolaou St, New Town ☎ 0241 97501/2

Colorado Entertainment Centre
A three-in-one choice for the dedicated. Go to the Colorado Pub for full-on rock, the Colorado Club for disco, techno and the latest sounds, and the Heaven Bar for simply relaxing.
✉ Orfanidou & Akti Miaouli St, New Town ☎ 0241 75120 Website: www.coloradoclub.gr 🕒 Late to early

Minuit Night Club
A good time venue located at the heart of the hotel district. Featuring international sounds playing alongside Greek folklore shows.
✉ 4 Kastellorizou St, New Town ☎ 0241 34647 🕒 Every night

Paradiso Dance Club
This is one of Rhodes' biggest and best-known nightclubs, located some way out of Rhodes Town on the west coast road. The club books international DJ stars, and you can be sure of hearing the latest European sounds.
✉ 1 G Seferi St ☎ 0241 62397 🕒 Every night

Faliráki

Reflexions
Big, lively venue playing soul, funk, disco and jazz. British DJs. Huge video/TV screen shows films and sport in afternoons in adjoining George's Bar.
✉ Faliráki ☎ 0241 86081

Theatre

Rhodes Town

Old Town Theatre
Greek folk dance sessions are staged during the season by the Nelly Dimoglou Theatre Company at this attractive venue.
✉ Andronicou St, Old Town (down lane on left of Municipal Baths) ☎ 0241 20157/29085 🕒 May–Oct, Mon, Wed, Fri 9:20PM

Rhodes Municipal Theatre
Stages an excellent programme of music, dance and theatre throughout the year, often featuring top performers. Well worth a visit even if you have little understanding of the Greek language. The music events especially, can be superb. Details from tourist information centres.
✉ Vasileos Georgiou I Square

Sound & Light Show
Popular recorded show telling the story of the Turkish siege of the city in 1522. Multilingual performances each night during the season, in English, German and French, with a weekly performance in Greek. Check at tourist information centres for times of performances.
✉ Gardens of the Palace of the Grand Masters, off Rimini Sq ☎ Box Office 0241 21922

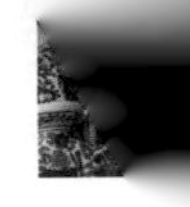

Sports and Watersports

Bowling

Rodos Bowling Hall
Small bowling alley and billiards centre.
60 Moschou H, Rhodes Town ☎ 0241 39852

Bungee Jumping

New World Extreme Sports Company
At Faliráki – where else? – the big orange towers of the bungee-jumping, sky-surfing, shriek-and-scream machine dominate the skyline. Billed as 45m of 'sheer terror'.
The Crane, Faliráki Beach, F

Cycling

Hellas Bike Hire
Bike hire and organised cycling trips.
Faliráki ☎ 0241 86777; mobile 0944 122119

Five-a-side Football

Astroturf five-a-side pitch attached to Happy Days Pool Bar. Pitch needs to be booked in advance and is best done as a group-booking of friends.
Líndos Avenue, Faliráki
☎ 0241 87438/86057

Go Karting

Located about 10km from Rhodes Town and 2km from Faliráki, this sizeable circuit has modern German-made karts.
Kartodrome Rodos, National Road ☎ 0241 86819

Golf

Afántou Golf Course
An 18-hole course of international standard; par 72. Clubs and pull cars are available for rent, and lessons are given.
Afántou ☎ 0241 51255; fax 51256

Tennis

Rhodes Tennis Club
Tennis may seem a hot option, but sea breezes will help you to keep cool.
4 N Sava, Elli Beach, New Town ☎ 0241 68090

Watersports

Dive Med
Based on a handsome old *caique* moored at Mandraki main road quay and offering trips along the coast to places such as Thérmes Kalithéa where there are permitted diving areas. Diving around the island shoreline is tightly controlled.
Mandraki Harbour
☎ 0241 33654; fax 0241 23780

Pro Surf Center Blue Horizon
Located behind the Blue Horizon Hotel at Ialyssós beach, this wind surfing centre caters for beginners to experienced surfers, including children. Expert tuition.
Ialyssós beach ☎ 0241 95819

Theo's Watersports Centre
Water skiing, paragliding, ringos and most other types of fun on the water.
Faliráki (near Apollo Beach Hotel) ☎ 0932 636405

Waterhoppers Diving Schools
Trips and dive training courses with experienced, qualified instructors. One-day introductory courses to more adventurous trips for the experienced. Operates from own boat. Family packages also available.
45 Kritika St, New Town
☎ & fax 0241 38146; mobile 0932 422617

Sun Safety

The sun is very strong in the summer so guard against sunburn. Crucial health reasons are the main concern, but you can also ruin your holiday if you have too much sun in the first day or two. Use reputable sun screening creams and ration your sunbathing carefully. Be especially careful not to expose young children to too much sun; ensure they wear hats and high protection creams.

What's On When

Easter

Easter is the major festival of the religious year. On Good Friday evening the church ceremonies begin in town and village, both inside the churches and outside as solemn processions move through the streets. On Holy Saturday night the most powerful ceremony takes place and culminates with great bursts of fireworks in the streets as Christ is declared 'risen'. People flow from the churches bearing lit candles which they try to keep alight until they reach home. There are early breakfast feasts on Sunday morning and then general feasting throughout the day. Churches are always packed but people gather outside as well. Remember to dress appropriately if you attend a church service.

Jan

6 Jan – Epiphany. Service in Cathedral of St John the Evangelist, Rhodes Town. Blessing of the sea water at Mandraki Harbour, when a priest throws a crucifix into the water and youngsters dive in for the honour of retrieving it

Feb–Mar

Pre-Lenten Carnival. During the weeks before the beginning of Lent, various carnivals are staged on Rhodes. Sunday before Lent: carnival processions and fancy dress in Rhodes Old Town and at Archángelos, Appolona, Afántou, Ialyssós, and Kameíros Skála. Following day: *Kathari Deftera*, 'Clean Monday', when families and friends head for the countryside and beaches to picnic and to fly kites.
7 Mar – Dodecanese Reunification Day. Celebrates reunification with Greece in 1947. Parade in Rhodes Town. Theatre performances.
25 Mar – Greek Independence Day.

Easter (date variable)

Most important festival of Greek Orthodoxy (➤ Panel). Expect explosive firecrackers over Easter weekend. Sými has its own very characteristic celebrations.

May

1 May – May Day. Country picnics; garlands of flowers brought back to decorate doorways and balconies.

Jun

24 Jun – Feast of St John the Baptist. Bonfires and parties.

Jul

First week of July – Naval Week. Concerts, fireworks and boat races.
20 Jul – Feast of Profítis Ilías. Large numbers of people assemble at the mountain of Profítis Ilías to celebrate feast day of Prophet Elijah.
30 Jul – Lively celebrations at the village of Soroni in honour of St Paul.

Aug

Dance festivals at various villages throughout the month.
6 Aug – Religious festival on Chálki; traditional mock battles, with throwing of flour and eggs.
15 Aug – Assumption (Dormition) of the Blessed Virgin Mary. Very important week-long festival, during which many Greeks return to their native island and village.

Sep

8 Sep – Birth of the Virgin. Unique event at Tsampíka, when women wishing to conceive make a special pilgrimage to the hilltop monastery church (➤ 67).

Oct

28 Oct – Ókhi Day ('No' Day). Patriotic celebration of Greece's refusal to capitulate to demands of Mussolini in 1940. Parades, folk dancing, speeches and general celebrations.

Nov

8 Nov – Feast of the Archangels Michael and Gabriel. Religious celebrations and festivities at Archángelos, and at monastery of Panormitis on the island of Sými .

Practical Matters

Above: *a Rhodian windmill*
Right: *a mounted policeman patrolling in Rhodes Old Town*

E DIFFERENCES

GMT	RHODES	Germany	USA (NY)	Netherlands	Spain
12 noon	2PM	1PM	7AM	1PM	1PM

BEFORE YOU GO

WHAT YOU NEED

● Required
○ Suggested
▲ Not required

Some countries require a passport to remain valid for a minimum period (usually at least six months) beyond the date of entry – contact their consulate or embassy or your travel agent for details.

	UK	Germany	USA	Netherlands	Spain
Passport	●	●	●	●	●
Visa (Regulations can vary – check before your journey)	▲	▲	▲	▲	▲
Onward or return ticket	▲	▲	▲	▲	▲
Health inoculations	○	○	○	○	○
Health documentation (reciprocal agreement, ➤ 91, Health)	●	●	●	●	●
Travel insurance	●	●	●	●	●
Driving licence (national or international)	●	●	●	●	●
Car insurance certificate (if own car)	●	●	●	●	●
Car registration document (if own car)	●	●	●	●	●

WHEN TO GO

Rhodes

High season

Low season

	JAN	FEB	MAR	APR	MAY	JUN	JUL	AUG	SEP	OCT	NOV	DEC
Season	Low	Low	Low	Low	High	High	High	High	High	Low	Low	Low
Temperature	12°C	12°C	15°C	18°C	23°C	28°C	30°C	29°C	27°C	22°C	18°C	13°C
Weather	Very wet	Wet	Sun/showers	Sun/showers	Sun	Sun	Sun	Sun	Sun	Sun/showers	Wet	Very wet

Very wet · Wet · Sun/showers · Sun

TOURIST OFFICES

In the UK
The National Tourist Organisation of Greece (NTOG)
4 Conduit Street
London W1R 0DJ
☎ 020 734 5997
Fax: 020 287 1369

In the USA
The National Tourist Organisation of Greece (NTOG)
645 Fifth Avenue
New York, NY10022
☎ (212) 421 577
Fax: (212) 826 6940

611 West Sixth Street
Suite 2198
Los Angeles
CA92668
☎ (213) 626 6696
Fax: (213) 489 9744

CONSULATES

UK	USA	Germany	Netherlands	Spain
(0241) 27306/ 27247	(01) 721 2951	(0241) 63730/ 29730	(0241) 31571/ 33577	(0241) 2246/ 22350

WHEN YOU ARE THERE

ARRIVING

Olympic Airways, ☎ (0241) 24571 and Aegean Airways ☎ (0241) 93860, operate flights daily between Athens and Rhodes. Flights to Crete and other main islands operate during summer months. Ferries operate throughout the year between Athens and Rhodes and there are ferry connections with other Dodecanese islands and with Crete and Turkey.

MONEY

Greece's currency is the euro, which is divided into 100 cents. Coins come in denominations of 1, 2, 5, 10, 20 and 50 cents and 1 and 2 euros. Notes come in denominations of 5, 10, 20, 50, 100 and 500 euros (the last two are rarely seen). American Express, Visa, MasterCard, Diners Club and other major credit cards are accepted in the larger and more expensive hotels, shops and restaurants, but otherwise cash is still the preferred method of payment in Rhodes.

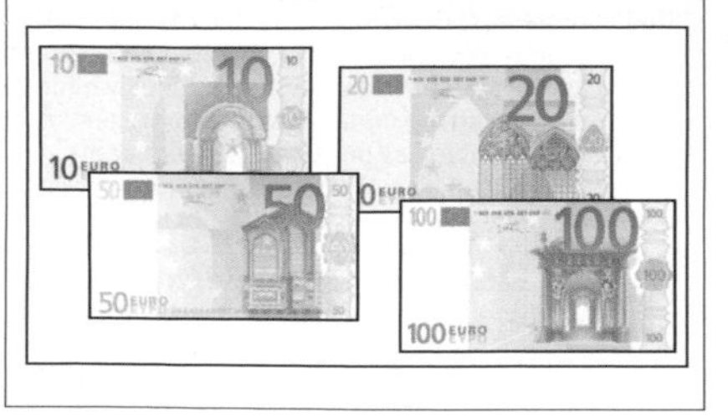

CUSTOMS

YES
Goods Obtained Duty Free outside the EU (Limits):
Alcohol (over 22% vol): 1L *or*
Alcohol (not over 22% vol): 2L
and Still table wine: 2L,
Cigarettes: 200 *or* Cigars: 50
or Tobacco: 250gms,
Perfume: 60ml,
Toilet water: 250ml
Goods bought Duty and Tax Paid for own use inside the EU (Guidance Levels):
Alcohol (over 22% vol): 10L
Alcohol (not over 22% vol): 20L *and* Wine 90L (max 60L sparkling): Beer: 100L
Cigarettes: 800, Cigars: 200, Tobacco: 1kg, Perfume and toilet water: no limit.
You must be 17 or over to benefit for alcohol and tobacco allowances.

NO

Drugs, firearms, ammunition, offensive weapons, obscene material, unlicensed animals.

OPENING HOURS

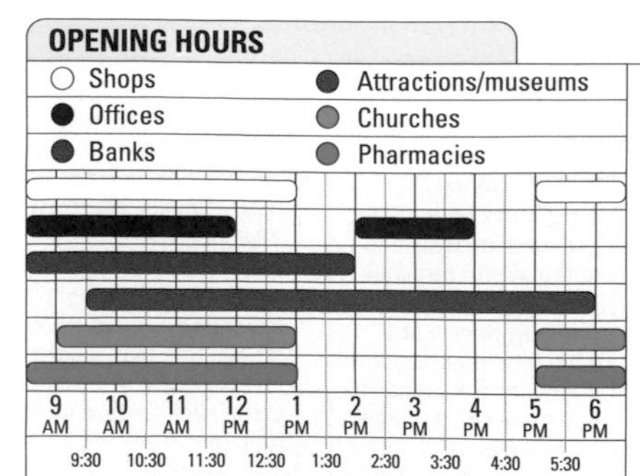

Supermarkets and gift shops, particularly in resorts, often stay open until 9 or 10PM. Pharmacies share a 24-hour rota system as indicated on all pharmacy windows. Rhodes Town Main Post Office, on Plateía Eleftherías, is open Mon–Fri 7AM–8PM. Check at tourist offices for opening hours of museums and attractions. Churches may stay open until 9PM.

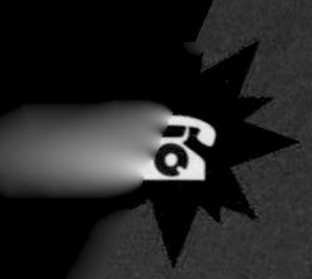

POLICE 100

FIRE 199

AMBULANCE 22222/25555

FOREST FIRE 191

DRIVE ON THE **RIGHT**

TOILETS ★★★

DRIVING (► 80)

Speed limit on national highways: **100kph**

Speed limit on main roads: **90kph**

Speed limit on minor roads: **50kph**

Must be worn in front seats and in the rear where fitted. Children under 10 years are not allowed in the front seat.

80 micrograms of alcohol in 100ml of breath is a criminal offence, and from 50 to 80 micrograms a civil offence. There is random breath testing.

Petrol (*venzini*) is usually available in five grades: super (*sooper*), regular (*apli*), unleaded (*amolyvdhi*), super unleaded (*sooper amolyvdhi*), and confusingly, *petrelaio*, which is diesel. Petrol stations are normally open 7–7 (closed Sun); larger ones (often self-service) are open 24hrs. Most take credit cards. There are few petrol stations in remote areas.

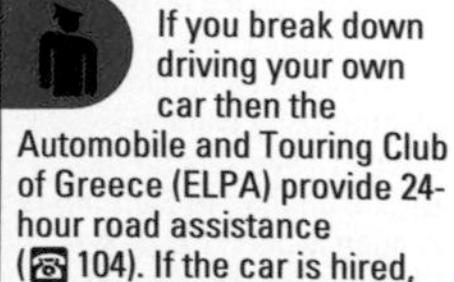

If you break down driving your own car then the Automobile and Touring Club of Greece (ELPA) provide 24-hour road assistance (☎ 104). If the car is hired, follow the instructions given in the documentation; most international rental firms provide a rescue service.

PUBLIC TRANSPORT

Internal Flights Domestic flights are operated by Olympic Airways ☎ (0241) 24571 and by Aegean Airways ☎ (0241) 93860. Domestic flight tickets are non-transferable. All flights are non-smoking. Flights are often well-booked in advance. Reserve seats in advance and confirm within five days of your flight.

Trains
There are no train services on Rhodes.

Buses The national bus company, KTEL (Kratiko Tamio Ellinikon Leoforion), serves the east coast of Rhodes from a bus stand in Papágou Street, just up from Rimíni Square. The municipal bus service RODA serves the west coast from a stand in Avérof Street behind the arcades of the New Market. There are timetables at the stand kiosks and tourist offices.

Boat Trips Ferries run between Rhodes Town and Pireás at least once a day (more often in summer). The trip can take up to 18 hours. Ferries run between Rhodes and the other Dodecanese islands and to Crete. Connections to the Cyclades are infrequent. Finding out about ferries can be frustrating, because rival agencies supply information only about the companies they represent. Ask at as many agencies as possible. Pleasure boats operate from Mandraki Harbour on day trips to Sými and Turkey and to various resorts, including Líndos.

Urban Transport Town buses Nos 2–6 leave from a stand opposite the main entrance to the New Market on Eleftherías. The town service is useful only if you wish to travel outside the immediate limits of the New Town and Old Town.

CAR RENTAL

Most of the leading car rental companies have offices in the main towns and at the airport terminal, and even resorts will probably have a few local hire firms. Car hire in Rhodes is expensive, however, and accident rates are high.

TAXIS

Central taxi rank in Rhodes Town is at Rimíni Square ☎ (0241) 27666. Call radio cabs on ☎ (0241) 64712/64734/64778. Boards indicating fares to main resorts and tourist sites are displayed at various points. Ask for fare tariff from tourist offices.

PHOTOGRAPHY

What to photograph: ancient sites (photography is free for hand held cameras on most) villages, parades, harbours. The Greek people also like being photographed, but it is polite to ask permission.
Where you need permission to photograph: in some museums and always if using a tripod. Never photograph near military installations.
Where to buy film: the most popular brands are available in all tourist areas. The sunlight is brilliant in summer and it is a good idea to use a lens filter.

TIPS/GRATUITIES

Yes ✓ No ✗

Restaurants (service not included)	✓	€1–2
Cafes/bars (service not included)	✓	€1
Tour guides	✓	€1–2
Taxis	✓	change
Porters	✓	€1
Chambermaids	✓	€1
Usherettes	✗	
Hairdressers	✓	€1
Cloakroom attendants	✓	€0.50
Toilets	✗	

HEALTH

Insurance
Nationals of EU and certain other countries can get medical treatment in Rhodes with the relevant documentation (Form E111 for Britons), although private medical insurance is still advised and is essential for other visitors.

Dental Services
Dental treatment is not available free of charge and should be covered by your personal medical insurance. Check with the Tourist Police or at your hotel for the name of the nearest dentist. Have a check-up before leaving home.

Sun Advice
Rhodes enjoys sunshine for most of the year, and from May until September it is almost constant. During July and August, when the sun is at it hottest, a hat, strong-protection suncream and plenty of water are recommended.

Drugs
Pharmacies (*farmakía*), indicated by a green cross sign, can give advice and prescriptions for common ailments. If you need prescription drugs, take the exact details from home. Most pharmacies have someone who can speak English.

Safe Water
Tap water is regarded as safe to drink. Bottled water is cheap to buy and is widely available. Drink plenty of water during hot weather.

PERSONAL SAFETY

Rhodes is safe generally, but crime is on the increase, especially in crowded places. Report any problems to the Tourist Police, who can often speak several languages.

- Leave money and valuables in your hotel safe.
- Carry only what you need and keep it hidden.

Tourist Police assistance:
☎ (0241) 23329/27423

TELEPHONES

International Direct Dialling is available throughout Rhodes. Calls can be made using a phone card in a telephone booth. Cards can be bought from kiosks, OTE offices and some shops.

International Dialling Codes

From Rhodes to:

UK:	**00 44**
Germany:	**00 49**
USA & Canada:	**00 49**
Netherlands:	**00 31**

POST

Post Offices are identified by a yellow 'OTE' sign. Shops and kiosks often sell stamps along with postcards. Post boxes are yellow. Post offices are generally open Mon–Friday 8–2.

ELECTRICITY

The power supply in Rhodes is 200 volts AC, 50 Hz. Sockets accept two-pin round plugs. Visitors from the UK require a plug adaptor and US visitors will need a transformer for appliances operating on 100–120 volts.

WHEN DEPARTING

- The airport departure tax is added to the price of your ticket when you purchase it.
- It is forbidden to export antiquities and works of art found in Rhodes.
- Allowances for exporting other goods may avary with the destination – check before departure.
- Confirm your flight times the day before departure.

LANGUAGE

The official language of Rhodes is Greek. Many of the locals speak English, but a few words of Greek can be useful in rural areas where locals may know no English. It is also useful to know the Greek alphabet – particularly for reading street names and road signs. A few useful words and phrases are listed below, with phonetic transliterations and accents to show emphasis. More words and phrases can be found in the AA *Essential Greek Phrase Book*. Because the method of translating Greek place-names has changed recently, some spellings may differ from older ones you find on the island.

English	Greek	English	Greek
hotel	*xenodhohío*	reservation	*to klisimo thesis*
bed and breakfast	*krevati ke proino*	room service	*to servis dhomátyo*
single room	*monó dhomátyo*		
double room	*dhipló dhomátyo*	chambermaid	*i kamariera*
		bath	*banío*
one person	*éna átoma*	shower	*dous*
one night	*éna nihte*	toilet	*toualéta*
money	*lefta*	travellers' cheque	*taxidhyotikí epitayí*
bank	*trápeza*		
exchange office	*ghrafío sinalágh-matos*	credit card	*pistotikí kárta*
		exchange rate	*isotimia*
		commission charge	*promothea*
post office	*tahidromío*		
coin	*kerma*	cashier	*tameas*
banknote	*hartonomisma*	change	*resta*
cheque	*epitayí*	passport	*dhiavatíryn*
café	*kafeteria*	waitress	*servitóra*
restaurant	*estiatorio*	starter	*mezédhes*
bar	*bar*	dessert	*epidhórpyo*
breakfast	*proino*	bill	*oghariasmó*
lunch	*yévma*	beer	*bíra*
dinner	*dhípno*	wine	*krasí*
table	*trapezi*	water	*neró*
waiter	*servitóros*	coffee	*kafés*
aeroplane	*aeropláno*	return ticket	*metepistrofís isitírio*
airport	*aerodhrómio*		
bus	*leoforío*	non-smoking	*mi kapnízondes*
boat	*plio*	street	*odos*
port	*limáni*	square	*plateía*
ticket	*isitírio*	car	*aftokínito*
single ticket	*apló isitírio*	petrol	*venzíni*
yes	*ne*	how are you?	*ti kánete?*
no	*ókhi*	do you speak English?	*milate Angliká?*
goodbye	*adío or yásas*		
please	*parakaló*	I don't understand	*then katalaveno*
thank you	*efharistó*		
hello	*yásas, yásoo*	how much?	*póso káni*
good morning	*kalí méra*	open	*aniktó*
good evening	*kalí spéra*	closed	*klistó*
good night	*kalí níkhta*	today	*símera*
excuse me	*ma sinchoríte*	tomorrow	*ávrio*

INDEX

Acknowledgements
The Automobile Assocation would like to thank the following photographers and libraries for their assistance in the preparation of this book:

MARY EVANS PICTURE LIBRARY 10b, **HULTON GETTY PICTURE COLLECTION** 10c, **INTERNATIONAL PHOTOBANK** 38b, **PICTURES COLOUR LIBRARY** 7c, **WORLD PICTURES** 7b. **www.euro.ecb.int/** 89.

The remaining photographs are held in the Association's own library (**AA PHOTOLIBRARY**) and were taken by Des Hannigan, with the exception of the following:

T L CARLSEN Front cover, a (pottery), Back cover (fish), 5a, 6a, 7a, 7d, 8a, 9a, 10a, 12b, 16b, 22b, 23a, 27c, 28b, 30b, 35b, 49b, 53b, 73a, 73b; **STEVE DAY** Front cover, b (Temple of Apollo), Front cover, c (folk dancer), Front cover, d (Thari Monastery, frescoes), 6b, 8b, 9c, 12c, 15b, 18/19, 19b, 19c, 21b, 31b, 37b, 38c, 44b, 53c, 58b, 68/69, 69b, 69c, 70a, 70b, 71b, 71c, 87a; **TERRY HARRIS** 62b; **KEN PATERSON** 63b.

Author's Acknowledgements
Des Hannigan wishes to thank friends and associates in Rhodes and Symi for their kindness and help. Special thanks to Mary Thymianou of the National Tourism Organisation of Greece in Rhodes Town, and to Antonios Bessas and Demetrios Polos of Gennádi, and Christos Fanarakis of Monólithos. Very special thanks to Tony Easton of Sými and to Wendy Wilcox and Nikos Halkitis. Thanks also to James Gibbons, Jennifer Roberts, Omer Singer,Tim Bar and John Flynn for their good company.

Managing editor: Jane Gregory **Copy editor**: Anne Heseltine

Dear Essential Traveller

Your comments, opinions and recommendations are very important to us. So please help us to improve our travel guides by taking a few minutes to complete this simple questionnaire.

You do not need a stamp (unless posted outside the UK). If you do not want to cut this page from your guide, then photocopy it or write your answers on a plain sheet of paper.

Send to: **The Editor, AA World Travel Guides, FREEPOST SCE 4598, Basingstoke RG21 4GY.**

Your recommendations...

We always encourage readers' recommendations for restaurants, nightlife or shopping – if your recommendation is used in the next edition of the guide, we will send you a ***FREE* AA *Essential* Guide** of your choice. Please state below the establishment name, location and your reasons for recommending it.

____

____

____

____

Please send me **AA *Essential*** ______________________________
(*see list of titles inside the front cover*)

About this guide...

Which title did you buy?
AA *Essential* ______________________________
Where did you buy it? ______________________________
When? m m / y y

Why did you choose an AA *Essential* Guide? ______________________________

____

____

____

____

Did this guide meet your expectations?
Exceeded ☐ Met all ☐ Met most ☐ Fell below ☐
Please give your reasons ______________________________

____

____

____

continued on next page...

Were there any aspects of this guide that you particularly liked? ______

______

______

______

Is there anything we could have done better? ______

______

______

______

______

About you...

Name (*Mr/Mrs/Ms*) ______

Address ______

______

______ Postcode ______

Daytime tel nos ______

Which age group are you in?

Under 25 ☐ 25–34 ☐ 35–44 ☐ 45–54 ☐ 55–64 ☐ 65+ ☐

How many trips do you make a year?

Less than one ☐ One ☐ Two ☐ Three or more ☐

Are you an AA member? Yes ☐ No ☐

About your trip...

When did you book? m m / y y When did you travel? m m / y y

How long did you stay? ______

Was it for business or leisure? ______

Did you buy any other travel guides for your trip?

If yes, which ones? ______

______

Thank you for taking the time to complete this questionnaire. Please send it to us as soon as possible, and remember, you do not need a stamp (*unless posted outside the UK*).

Happy Holidays!

The AA and the Automobile Association Limited, their subsidiaries and any other companies or bodies in which either has an interest ('the AA Group') may use information about you to provide you with details of other products and services, by telephone or in writing. The AA Group as a matter of policy does not release its lists to third parties.

If you do not wish to receive further information please tick the box... ☐